Speeches
For Every
Occasion

Speeches For Every Occasion!

Shortcuts to Effective Public Speaking

David & Ruth Belson

CITADEL PRESS
Kensington Publishing Corp.
www.kensingtonbooks.com

CITADEL PRESS BOOKS are published by

Kensington Publishing Corp.
850 Third Avenue
New York, NY 10022

All Kensington titles, imprints, and distributed lines are available at special quantity discounts for bulk purchases for sales promotions, premiums, fund-raising, educational, or institutional use. Special book excerpts or customized printings can also be created to fit specific needs. For details, write or phone the office of the Kensington special sales manager: Kensington Publishing Corp., 850 Third Avenue, New York, NY 10022, attn: Special Sales Department, phone 1-800-221-2647.

First Kensington printing: November 2002

10 9 8 7 6 5 4 3 2 1

Printed in the United States of America

Cataloging data may be obtained by the Library of Congress.

ISBN 0-8065-2428-6

INTRODUCTION

The purpose of this book is to make participation in all organizations—civic, church, school, veterans' and other group activities—easy and enjoyable. Models and form-books are used by lawyers, and the inexperienced participant in club work also should have patterns to follow. This book offers no explanations to wade through, but illustrates the common situations the user might be called upon to meet. An opportunity to study public ceremonies by example will afford the user the courage to face a task often regarded as an ordeal. Many members and officers of organizations tread a path new to them when they plan a meeting, testimonial dinner, charity drive, or memorial service, or when they take part in any one or more of the public events which this work exemplifies. The user, of course, must adapt the forms to his special needs.

The forms are divided into two sections. Those which concern community, religious, school, fraternal, club, political or other group activities are in Section I. Those of special interest to labor organizations are in Section II.

The names of persons and organizations whenever used in the models are fictitious.

The use of the models should result in more productive

programs, happier participants and audiences. The book is intended as a time-saver for the busy participant in public events and as an aid for the less experienced.

Many of these model ceremonies have been tested in the public arena by the authors, David Belson, an Assistant Attorney General on my staff, and his wife Ruth, a speech instructress.

LOUIS J. LEFKOWITZ
Attorney General of the State of New York

Contents

Section II EXAMPLES OF LABOR
UNION CEREMONIES

Speeches For Every Occasion

Section I

EXAMPLES OF PUBLIC CEREMONIES
FOR CIVIC, FRATERNAL, RELIGIOUS,
PATRIOTIC, VETERANS' AND OTHER
GROUP ACTIVITIES

1. Organizing a Speakers' Club

I am happy to have a part in these proceedings. They will start you on your way to enjoying the benefits of membership in a Speakers' Club.

The Speakers' Clubs, International, is an organization of men and women interested in personal growth and development through training in speech and leadership. New chapters are welcomed and are continually being formed, extending the benefits of membership to other fields and to new groups of men and women. We of the Speakers' Clubs, International, welcome you and wish you well. I now call upon Mr. James Brown, District Service Manager of the International body, to present the charter which will empower you to function as an affiliate.

PRESENTING CHARTER

After careful investigation of your petition for a charter to the Speakers' Clubs, International, your application has been approved. The Grand President has instructed me to form you into a chapter. It therefore gives me great pleasure to present to you the charter which permits you to function as a chapter of the Speakers' Clubs, International. The charter has been duly signed by the International officers.

In turning it over to you, permit me to say that you who have been instrumental in the formation of this chapter have undertaken an important task. Membership in this organization of ambitious men and women is a privilege combined with responsibility. In every community there are men and women who will welcome the chance to obtain such training when it is made available. Members of our Clubs will be found in public office, in the ranks of industry, in labor, in organizations of all kinds and among the leading business and professional men.

You are now a duly constituted chapter of the Speakers' Clubs, International. The future of this chapter is the responsibility of its members. Be watchful of the character of those who seek admission, and if admitted, give them proper instruction, and conduct the business of your chapter in accordance with the constitution and by-laws of the International.

By virtue of the dispensation granted by the Speakers' Clubs, International, I will proceed to install the officers so that they may function as the administrators of a duly constituted chapter of Speakers' Clubs, International. At the conclusion of the installation ceremonies, I will turn over the gavel to your President. He will open the meeting and proceed to business. I congratulate you on your enterprise in forming this chapter. We welcome you and hope you will thrive and prosper.

CLOSING

I express the hope that this newly formed Speakers' Club will endure, for it has a useful purpose. It can be an enterprise for much good. It will serve you and those yet to come. The training you will receive here will add to your capacity for leadership in the community, in your professions, in your lodges and clubs. It will provide opportunities for lasting friendships.

Membership in this Club means assuming an obligation to attend meetings and to undertake and perform all assignments with diligence and sincerity. It requires research to prepare for the assignments. It requires an understanding of community problems and national affairs. It aids the development of hobbies and cultural interests.

I bid you farewell and the best of luck in your new enterprise.

2. Organizing a Camera Club

OPENING

I very much appreciate the honor of presiding at this event. My purpose is to explain the function of the

P.A.L. Camera Clubs. We will also take the opportunity to extol a worthy and unselfish worker who has supervised the Camera Clubs in this area and to honor him with a citation of merit.

The P.A.L. Camera Clubs have been functioning without fanfare for several years and have achieved excellent results. The work of the Camera Clubs is carried on by donations of money and photographic equipment by public-spirited citizens and organizations. We also conduct area-wide contests in which boys and girls receive prizes of equipment they need to pursue their hobby.

APPEALING FOR FUNDS

The Camera Clubs have been accomplishing much good. We can, of course, use financial help and we are in urgent need of volunteer workers. We invite men and women to offer their services and to donate photographic equipment toward making good citizens of our kids. The Council of Camera Clubs, which coordinates the activities of the Camera Clubs, is a fine organization. It includes in its membership 100 clubs in this area. It conducts contests and, as needed, supplies judges and lecturers. It is also a clearing house for inter-club information. In general, it serves as a sort of "big brother" to the clubs.

The P.A.L. Camera Clubs is an undertaking worth knowing about and supporting, especially in these days of youth problems. Children who participate in the organization's activities learn to get along well with the police, acquire a respect for the rights of others, and are given a good start to becoming good citizens. The P.A.L.

Clubs offer a particularly attractive solution to some of the major problems of juvenile delinquency.

INTRODUCING PRESENTER OF GIFT

You will next hear from one who has attained success in business and has used it to help others. He has been active in the field of vocational guidance and has given large sums of money and expended much energy in developing and strengthening the Camera Clubs. He is always available when needed. He seeks no glory. His one concern is the prosperity of the club. I present Mr. Richard Ross, who will make a presentation to our guest of honor, Mr. Sam Smith.

PRESENTING THE CITATION

It is fitting that we pay tribute to a man who has devoted himself so completely to the service of the community. He has done and is still doing a competent job as president of the P.A.L. Camera Council. To every position he holds, he gives everything he has. He is always on his toes devising something new to sustain interest in the clubs. He devotes his time without the slightest thought of compensation other than the satisfaction of seeing boys and girls become interested and proficient in so wholesome a hobby. He does much to give the young people a sense of belonging, of having responsibilities and of being wanted.

Sam Smith, you have been a great benefactor of our clubs and a real friend to the many kids who are members. You have been especially helpful in getting children interested in the Camera Club. The community owes you a vote of thanks for all you have done—for your hard, conscientious and successful work.

I am happy, therefore, to present to you this citation which reads:

> "For outstanding qualities of leadership, initiative, and service to Police Athletic League Camera Clubs and for distinguished service in encouraging good citizenship practices among our youth."

This citation is the greatest honor that we can confer. It is given for outstanding service to the clubs. You deserve this honor.

INTRODUCING GUEST OF HONOR

I am pleased to present our guest of honor. He has devoted himself conscientiously and successfully to the field of youth guidance. Mr. Sam Smith.

THANKING SPEAKERS

Thank you for the warm tributes and the citation. I hope a set speech is not expected of me. However, you have the right to an expression of my thanks and appreciation. I do fully appreciate all that has been said and done here.

I am glad to have been of service to the members of the P.A.L. Camera Clubs. I consider it a most worthy cause. I believe the Clubs have been a very important factor in helping the youngsters. In these Clubs the community has a powerful means of preventing boys and girls from going astray. The Clubs perform a most useful function and deserve the united support of the community.

May I add that it takes money and supplies to maintain the projects. It would be nice if the next time our guests are in a camera shop they would buy an extra roll of film or a package of enlarging paper for our clubs. And if anyone has an extra camera to donate it would be put to good use by some club member. I can think of no better way to make some teenager a bit happier.

CLOSING

In bringing this meeting to a close it is with a feeling that we have accomplished much good. We have, I trust, brought home to the community leaders who are present the value of the P.A.L. Camera Clubs. They have been a successful way of providing youngsters with wholesome environmental conditions and of teaching them a satisfying and profitable hobby. The energies of youth can be directed to paths away from trouble. The youth of the community need your help. The teenager in this country is at the crossroads. He can go down the unhappy path of waywardness or he can have his energy concentrated on wholesome activity. With your help we shall direct him along the latter road. Money is important; even more important is your participation.

3. Organizing a Civic Association

OPENING BY TEMPORARY CHAIRMAN

We are embarking upon an important undertaking—the formation of an association of residents to protect and advance our interests and to stimulate participation in the civic affairs of our community. We cannot hope to be successful working individually, but by combining our efforts, maximum results can be obtained. We all have a desire to achieve a richer life and a better community. We have every hope that our common goal will be attained. This association of neighbors, now in the process of formation, needs your support, particularly at this stage of its development.

NOMINATION AND ELECTION OF OFFICERS

The first step in forming a group is to elect a president. Nominations are now in order. (*A motion is made to nominate John Jones for president. Thereupon, it is regularly moved and seconded that nominations be closed.*)

There being no objection, nominations are closed and we shall proceed to vote. Please indicate your choice on the blank slips which are being handed out. (*Balloting proceeds and votes are counted.*)

The result of the balloting is the unanimous election of John Jones. I therefore declare John Jones our first president. Mr. Jones will now assume the chair. (*Temporary chairman retires.*)

PRESIDENT'S ACCEPTANCE

Thank you for the honor of the presidency. I assure you that I appreciate it deeply. Nothing could give me greater satisfaction than to be chosen to head an organization of my neighbors. There are many matters of great concern to our community, and it is reassuring to know that there is a group such as this to represent and speak for it.

NOMINATION AND ELECTION OF SECONDARY OFFICERS

We will now proceed to the nomination and election of the officers of vice-president, secretary, treasurer and an Executive Board of ten members, five to serve for two years and five to serve for one year. (*A motion is made to cast a single ballot for the unanimous election of the entire slate. The motion is then seconded.*)

A motion has been made and seconded to cast a single ballot for the unanimous election of the slate submitted by the Nominating Committee. I hereby instruct the secretary to cast a single ballot for the unanimous election of the persons nominated. (*Ballot is cast.*)

The secretary having cast a ballot for the unanimous election of the slate, I hereby declare the persons nominated to be elected to their respective offices.

APPOINTING COMMITTEE TO DRAFT CONSTITUTION

I will appoint three members to draft a constitution and I instruct them to report at the next meeting. (*Three members are designated.*)

ADJOURNING MEETING

If there is no objection, the meeting will be adjourned. Hearing none, the meeting stands adjourned.

4. Installing Officers

OPENING

We are about to perform one of the most important ceremonies attaching to our membership in the Speakers' Club—the installation of the newly elected officers.

The Speakers' Club is a non-profit organization which is designed to stimulate interest in and promote the art of cultural expression; it trains men and women in leadership; it stimulates and develops a greater interest in the art of public speaking. It is strictly non-sectarian and non-partisan.

The Speakers' Club is more than an organization. It is a faith—a belief in democracy, a belief that men and women can assemble from different interests and occupations, from different social and economic conditions, and unite for educational purposes and self-improvement.

INTRODUCING INSTALLING OFFICER

The installing officer is a Past President of the Speakers' Club, Charles Carter.

INSTALLING PRESIDENT

You have been chosen to preside over the destinies of the Speakers' Club for the ensuing year. The president is the most important person in any organization, for upon him rests the duty of seeing that the club moves forward and prospers. The honor of leadership carries responsibilities with it. The office is looked upon as a distinction and an honor, but it is primarily a post of service. You have won the confidence of the members and have been entrusted with this responsibility. You have been chosen as the person most able to give effective leadership. The president's obligation is to inspire our members, preserve peace and harmony, and lead the club to success and accomplishment. A successful president is firm, competent, tactful and just. As I pass the gavel of your office to you, may I say that you possess all these qualifications and that you have earned the honor. I have every confidence that you will have a successful administration. The gavel is now yours. With it goes a warm welcome to our new leader and a pledge from every member to work with you toward ever higher achievements.

INSTALLING VICE-PRESIDENT

Mr. Vincent Vale, our new Vice-President: The by-laws of the Speakers' Club require the vice-president to perform all the duties of the president in his absence and to assume the chair whenever he so requests. You are familiar with the powers and responsibilities of the president. Those powers and responsibilities are also yours. Your fellow members have found in you capabilities which will help our new president with the difficult and time-consuming tasks before him. We know you will be ever ready to assist him in performing his obligations.

INSTALLING TREASURER

Mr. Fred Fund, our new Treasurer: You are the guardian, the watchdog, of our funds. It is your duty prudently to manage the funds of the Club. The skillful performance of your duties is of the greatest importance to the welfare and the prosperity of the organization.

INSTALLING SECRETARY

The secretary's duties are substantially of a business character and are important to the welfare of the Club. Without a competent secretary the wheels of the Club would grind to a sudden stop. Punctuality in attendance at the meeting of the Club is an indispensable requisite of the secretary. He should be first in his place at its meetings and the nature of his duties is such that he can scarcely avoid being the last to leave the meeting room. He is particularly charged with the duty of watching the proceedings of the Club and making a complete record of all things proper to be recorded; to keep the financial accounts between the Club and its members; to receive all monies due the Club and pay them into the hands of the treasurer; to prepare the annual reports, and to perform all other duties pertaining to the office as may be ordered by the president.

Your reports and minutes constitute the Club's current history. The secretary records the business transacted at all meetings and is the custodian of all documents and records. Your skill, understanding, and judgment are well known to the members and we are sure the performance of the duties of your new office will make us even prouder of you.

INSTALLING EXECUTIVE BOARD

Board members are chosen for their qualifications of leadership, for upon them depend the future strength and success of the organization. Membership on the Board is an honor and privilege and with it come responsibilities. The function of the Board is to look after the affairs of the organization between meetings. The Board is the team—the president, its captain.

ACCEPTANCE BY PRESIDENT

Thank you very much for the great honor you have conferred upon me. It is an honor of which any man may be proud. The roll of the ex-presidents of the Speakers' Club is an illustrious one. I have but two ambitions during my term of office: One is that I may be able to do as everyone of my predecessors has done, that is, leave the Club at the close of my term of office stronger and better than it was at the beginning; and my second ambition, that I may be able to call you all one year from tonight, as I do not hesitate to call you all now, my personal friends.

CLOSING

In accepting leadership of the Speakers' Club, you, the new officers and board members, have dedicated yourselves to the service of the members. Your choice as officers is a manifestation of the esteem in which you are held. We rejoice with you today. The members pledge to work untiringly at your side. I am confident that officers and members will continue to meet their responsibilities with courage, with faith, and with vision.

5. The Birthday Testimonial

OPENING

I know of no one more deserving of this celebration than is Chester Chase. Yet Chester has little desire for personal acclaim. When he was told about plans for celebrating his seventieth birthday he was reluctant to approve. What induced him to go along with the plans was the hope that through it some of the humanitarian enterprises he has been supporting would be helped. Over a period of thirty years he has set an example of public service—particularly in the field of mental health. He had farsighted views of the needs and potentialities in the field long before mental illness became recognized as our number one health problem.

Chester Chase's achievements will inspire others to serve the mentally and physically disabled, and the community.

INTRODUCING PRESENTOR OF AWARD

It is appropriate that the Chairman of the Board of Directors of the Association be the first speaker to pay tribute to our guest of honor. I present Mr. Stanford Start.

BIRTHDAY TRIBUTE AND PRESENTATION OF AWARD

Seventy years young—and I mean young, for there are few half your age who are as alert, understanding, helpful and wise as you are today. If you look backward, you can be proud of the role you've taken in community life these last thirty years. But if you look ahead, you must realize that your wisdom will find many beneficial occasions for use. You have the vigor of men half your age and the wisdom that, at any age, comes to very few.

I count it a pleasure and an honor to be permitted to pay homage to you for your public service. You are a warm human being who has used his gifts and worldly possessions for the good of humanity. You have given much happiness to all those who have touched your life. May you have many more birthdays on which we can toast you!

I have a little token for you. Because we love you it takes the form of a loving cup. It is engraved:

> "To Chester Chase in grateful recognition and with deep appreciation for all he has done in advancing the well-being of our community."

Your capacity for friendship and your love for your fellow-man is great. Your life has been strenuous and full. What you have achieved has been by your own labor and efforts.

It is a pleasure to say "Happy Birthday" to you. The community could well use *another* seventy years of such greatness as yours. My birthday wish is that you may be with us for many years to come so that we may all benefit from your passion for service.

It is with extreme pleasure that I present you with this loving cup.

INTRODUCING COLLEAGUE

I wish to present to you a colleague of our guest of honor. He is connected with many institutions which have as their object the relief of suffering. He is president of the Hope Hospital and a member of the board of directors of many other hospitals and institutions. He is a public-spirited and useful citizen who has devoted much time and energy to educational, charitable and religious interests—Mr. Charles Sindex.

BIRTHDAY TRIBUTE

I welcome the opportunity to express my admiration and warm personal regard for Chester. I've enjoyed and appreciated his friendship for many years and I hope to for many years to come. I join with his host of friends and admirers in this tribute to him on the occasion of his seventieth birthday. He has been before the public in a prominent and useful way so long that he seems to constitute a permanent institution. If he ever had a selfish motive that actuated his service I never knew it. I know of no one who has contributed more than he has to the welfare of our community. Chester Chase's nobility of purpose, his wisdom and devotion to the community's welfare, have earned him the admiration of everyone. At a time when some tired young men are trying to force all men and women to retire at sixty-five, Chester Chase at seventy completes another year of usefulness to his community and pleasure to his friends. It is a constant source of amazement to me how one man in only seventy short years has done so much for so many. He has not only made an invaluable contribution to the community, but by his warm personality, generosity, and loyalty he has enriched the lives of his many friends. He has given lavishly of his many talents and resources.

It is a great joy to salute him on his seventieth birthday. I hope for many more years of association with him.

INTRODUCING GUEST OF HONOR

I have had the privilege of knowing Chester Chase for a good many years and my admiration and affection for him grow with time. Those of us who have the privilege of knowing him realize why he stands for everything that is good and wonderful in our community. I will call upon him to respond. Our guest of honor, Chester Chase.

THANKS AND APPRECIATION

Thank you very much for your very gracious and generous remarks and for your wonderful tributes. I wish I could find the words to tell you the great joy that is mine today, but any words, no matter which I might choose, would not be adequate to describe my happiness at this moment. Your faith and confidence in me will always be a source of inspiration and an added stimulus for me to continue my efforts to render service. To all my loyal friends who have made these years so happy and so fruitful, I wish to express my heartfelt thanks.

I convey my deep appreciation to you, Mr. Ford, for presiding so ably at these ceremonies. To Mr. Start my thanks for the excellent presentation and to all of you for your kind sentiments.

Much as I would like to prolong this happy moment, I will close with the prayer that the "Creator of all mankind grant me the wisdom, the strength of heart and mind to serve this community for years to come." Bless you all.

CLOSING

Before concluding, I will read several congratulatory messages I received for our guest of honor:

CONGRATULATORY MESSAGES

"I welcome this opportunity to congratulate my friend Chester Chase on his seventieth birthday. He has made an invaluable contribution to his community by his public service. I join with his many friends in wishing him happy days and many more birthdays.

Robert Church"

"Please convey my felicitations to Mr. Chester Chase on the occasion of his seventieth birthday. Mr. Chase's devotion to his community's welfare merits the tributes he is receiving.

Edward Clarke"

"It is a real pleasure to send a message of congratulations to you. Your interest in community welfare and your dedication to helping those who need help mark you as a truly great human being. In this spirit let us say 'Many happy returns of the day.'

Herbert Horton"

"The accomplishments and contributions of Chester Chase more than deserve the testimonial tendered to him by a grateful community on the occasion of his seventieth birthday. Our affectionate birthday wishes to him.

Mr. & Mrs. Seymour Stanton"

We are fortunate indeed that Chester Chase has been able to devote a lifetime to the service of the community and, selfishly, but with great affection, we hope that he will continue to serve with us for many years to come.

6. Testimonial to a Journalist

OPENING

Freedom of the press, one of the most cherished corner-stones of our American heritage, was won before the Declaration of Independence. In 1773 John Peter Zenger, a New York printer, was imprisoned for taking issue with the British governor. Zenger's acquittal in a celebrated trial firmly established the precedent for a free and independent press in this land.

Today, we honor Roy Ralson for his efforts in preserving this heritage, for defending our liberty, for upholding our democratic principles, for helping to keep our press free, for his skillful and accurate reporting of news. For all of these qualities he has been rightfully called the dean of reporters.

It is a great satisfaction to see that his wide knowledge,

ability, and devotion to public service are recognized by
the tender of this testimonial.

INTRODUCING JOURNALIST

To present an award to our guest of honor, we have
with us a newspaperman whose honest interpretation of
the news is known and respected by thousands. Many of
us have benefited from his clear and interesting accounts
of important happenings of our times. He is a fearless
champion of all that is good and right. Mr. Howard
Hester.

PRESENTING AWARD

Every citizen of this community owes you a debt for
the high civic service you have rendered to it. You have
found time, despite exacting newspaper duties, to give
the benefit of your talents to welfare agencies. You are
endowed with a fine mind, cultivated by unusual opportunities for mingling with people of distinction. Your
untiring industry, your sound sense and unswerving
fidelity have attracted attention. Your achievements are
the result of inherent strength of character and intelligent
application.

The Sun-Journal is establishing a Roy Ralson Award
for distinguished service to journalism to be given to
members of the organization who show unusual enterprise and initiative. You are the first to receive such an
award. We recognize fully the service you have rendered
to our organization. No one deserves the plaque more
than you do. Therefore, on behalf of the Sun-Journal

organization it is my privilege to present to you the Roy Ralson Award for truly outstanding work and distinguished service; for your contribution to humanity through journalism; for your fight for the elimination of discrimination by reason of race or creed; for your reputation as a fearless fighter for the good of the people. There are few who would state the truth more bluntly or with less fear of consequences—or shout it louder—than you.

This event also gives the public an opportunity to recognize the efforts of their local newspapermen—those hardworking craftsmen who regularly channel into the lives about them the most important and humanly interesting happenings of the times. The role of the press as an agency of public education is an important one. Newspaper Week deserves to be universally observed.

I am happy to pay this tribute to you. It is a great privilege for me to salute so distinguished a journalist, the dean of newspapermen.

INTRODUCING GUEST OF HONOR

I now present the man you have been waiting to hear. Roy is favorably known to public officials, diplomats, and correspondents abroad and at home. His warm personality and capacity for friendship serve him well in gathering news and the development of news sources. He is a man of great qualities—integrity, balance, common sense, courage, simplicity. He has had long experience in public life and many contacts with world statesmen. He has political knowhow and considerable popular appeal. His many years with the Sun-Journal have helped the newspaper attain a position of great prestige and influence. And now our guest of honor, Roy Ralson.

THANKS AND APPRECIATION

I am deeply touched that so many have done me the honor of coming out tonight. I want to thank you at the outset, Mr. Jameson, for the wonderful way in which you have presided at this testimonial dinner. I deem it a very great honor to be the first recipient of the Roy Ralson Award. Please don't get the idea that you owe me anything. I enjoyed the various positions I held with the paper through the years. I have been happy in my work.

I have written a few remarks for this occasion but no script can prepare one for the emotions I feel at this moment. It is difficult to find words to express my thanks for the kind thoughts, the confidence in me, that was expressed tonight. The tributes are pleasing, but at the same time they serve to emphasize the great responsibility that will be mine to live up to.

William Shakespeare, who obviously found himself as hard-put as I am now for words to match your kind sentiments, said:

"I can no other answer make but thanks
And thanks, and ever thanks. . . ."

And thus "thanks and thanks and ever thanks" for the kindness you have shown me—for the confidence you have placed in me.

Everything that has been said about Roy Ralson has been well said. We all wish him happiness, and it is our fervent hope that the honor and happiness which he and his family are now enjoying may continue and increase for the rest of his days.

7. Testimonial to a Musician

WELCOME

We welcome you to this concert of Beethoven's music. The intermission in the program will give us an opportunity to honor one who has given outstanding and distinguished service to thousands of music lovers by making these summer concerts available to them. I refer, of course, to Mr. Whitney Wilson who for many years has encouraged talent of every race, color, and creed. He has brought us good music and has given encouragement to gifted artists, known and unknown. He has always maintained great zest for musical performances and is not jaded or weary of concert-going.

Music is the universal line of communication linking us as citizens with one another. It speaks to us in terms which transcend the boundaries of any one group. The times in which we live call for the strengthening of every bond of unity while we respect our differences. Music is but another expression of the eternal effort of man to enrich himself and his world.

INTRODUCING SPEAKER FOR PRESENTATION

To make the presentation of the scroll we have chosen an artist whose great natural talents have stirred and inspired all audiences privileged to see and hear him. We have enjoyed his performance before the intermission and we are confident that you will enjoy his numbers following the ceremony. I am justifiably proud to introduce Mr. Martin Menuhan who will present the scroll to our guest of honor, Mr. Whitney Wilson.

PRESENTATION OF SCROLL

The privilege of presenting Mr. Whitney Wilson with a scroll for outstanding service to music lovers has been given to me. Mr. Wilson has a passionate love for music and the people who make it. I could not say of Whitney Wilson any more nor any better than is said in this scroll, which I will read:

"In recognition of distinguished service in the cause of brotherhood and for the good music you have brought us, as well as for the many gifted artists you have started on their way to notable careers. With music as a catalytic agent you have demonstrated harmony and brotherhood—interfaith in action. One of your chief benefactions is the School of Music for which you paid most of the building cost. In addition you contributed heavily to its endowment and scholarship funds. You have encouraged young talent who otherwise might never have been heard or seen; you have given your audiences music of a multitude of origins; you have fostered live music, promoted greater appreciation of the musical arts, and created an atmosphere in which the musical arts and artists will be given recognition and appreciation locally and nationally."

THANKS AND APPRECIATION

Will you allow me first to say how greatly I appreciate the courtesy and honor which you have done me this evening. How can I convey the full measure of my appreciation for this beautiful scroll? I am grateful for your kindness and thoughtfulness in presenting it to me. I am deeply touched and all I am able to say at the moment is, thank you very much.

CLOSING

This large audience is a tribute to the continuing appeal of music and to the personal popularity of Mr. Wilson. Before concluding, I would like to express my appreciation, and I am sure the appreciation of the audience and thousands throughout the State, for Mr. Wilson's distinguished services to music lovers.

There has been a tremendous growth in musical in-

terest and activity in the past fe
growth Mr. Wilson has played an i
is no formula for producing genius, but at least we can
create an environment in which men and women of
great talent can flourish. It is to this environment that
Mr. Wilson contributes so much. We salute Mr. Wilson
and wish him many more fruitful years.

8. Testimonial to a Woman Civic Leader

OPENING

I have the privilege of greeting you who are here to
honor Mary Charlton—a woman devoted to the cause of
service. Testimonials to men are commonplace occur-
rences. Paying homage to women is much less usual.

Not too long ago American women had no constitutional
right to vote. With the ratification of the Fifteenth
Amendment there emerged a steady demand for the en-
franchisement of women. As a parallel to this political
movement, women commenced to find intellectual interests outside their homes. Women's organizations have
exerted a distinct influence on the affairs of community,
state, and nation.

Thus, the myth of the weaker sex has been dispelled.

Leadership by women in national and world affairs, once restricted, is now general. The old limitations on women's participation no longer exist. More women are holding elective public office than ever before. More women are in the forefront of humanitarian endeavor.

INTRODUCING SPEAKER

Our speaker's deep interest in world peace, education, and human relations has earned her many awards and honorary degrees. She is editor of a magazine for career women. She is in great demand as a lecturer on world events. She strongly favors women's participation in public affairs. Through her keen and comprehensive interpretation of world events, she has stimulated many women to do their share in weaving a world pattern. All of these combine to make her a most useful citizen and the right person to make the presentation of a citation of merit to our guest of honor, Mrs. Charlton. I am honored to introduce Mrs. Mary Baldwin.

TRIBUTES

Mrs. Charlton has demonstrated in many ways her sincere interest in the welfare of the community. The community, in turn, has recognized her administrative abilities and the high quality of her leadership. She has been marked for honors. Public housing is just one of many projects in which she is engaged. She is recognized as a spokesman for civil liberties, and she is widely hailed as an ardent advocate of harmonious relations among our many races and nationalities.

Mrs. Charlton is truly one of the great women of our State. Her grace and wisdom are equaled only by the courageous determination with which she strives for a better life for people everywhere. Though known as a pioneer in many fields of public service, her greatest devotion is to the low-income class for whom she zealously works to bring about proper shelter and a better standard of living. There is no field of human service to which she does not bring her deep concern and compassion. All agencies serving the troubled among us owe her a debt of gratitude that can be fulfilled only by carrying forward the things she believes in and cherishes.

We salute her for her years of devotion to the community and her very real influence in guiding the welfare agencies. She has been a mighty worker for all humanitarian causes. She has brought courage and new hope to literally thousands of underprivileged and needy persons. It is a pleasure to say to Mrs. Charlton: "Well done! You have been a leader in the fight for recognition of the rights of the individual."

Mrs. Charlton, you have been, and are, one of the outstanding personalities in the pioneering and development of the program for low-cost housing for those who need it most. Your presence and guiding spirit have been an inspiration to those who work with you. You have brought to every organization in which you are interested a broad and generous understanding gained in your many years of leadership in social work. Your zest and vision are always available for causes that would better our community. You are a woman of rare intelligence, grace, and integrity, and richly deserve the glowing praise you have received today.

It is my honor to present you with this citation which reads:

> "For a lifetime of service to humanity and for her example of courage, faith, and triumph over many obstacles. She has magnificently fostered the dignity of mankind in her successful efforts to obtain proper housing for minority groups."

INTRODUCING GUEST OF HONOR

Our guest of honor is extraordinary for the range of her interests. Among those interests, in addition to housing, are: religious, philanthropic, and social welfare activities, the problems of youth, education, health, hospitals, good government and politics. It is my great pleasure to present, Mrs. Charles Charlton.

ACCEPTANCE

I accept this high honor with gratitude. I accept it not so much in my individual capacity as on behalf of the many civic, educational, and religious groups which bore the brunt of the campaign for slum clearance and low-cost housing. My heartfelt thanks to you all for coming here to pay these magnificent compliments and encomiums.

CLOSING

Mrs. Charlton, who has done so much for the betterment of her own neighborhood, shares the vision of an even greater country, the vision described long ago by Walt Whitman:

> Fresh come, to a new world indeed, yet long
>   prepared,
> I see the genius of the modern, child of the
>   real and ideal,
> Clearing the ground for broad humanity, the
>   true America, heir of the past so grand,
> To build a grander future.

9. Testimonial to a Philanthropist

OPENING

It is a pleasure to pay tribute to Richard Stone who has been in the forefront of all communal endeavors. He has dedicated his superb talents to the furtherance of human welfare. He is a founder, director, and general benefactor of the Mercy Hospital and one of the mainstays of the institution. His great interest and steady counsel have been a constant source of strength. He is a leader in many other charitable endeavors and has a long and brilliant record of support and active participation on behalf of the sick, aged, and troubled.

We are proud to have such a man among us—happy to pay him honor. His sympathetic understanding of civic needs, his vision and attainments, have enriched our community. This dinner is for the purpose of expressing our heartfelt thanks to Richard Stone for the inspiration of his example.

INTRODUCING PRESENTOR OF CITATION

I introduce one who is unremitting in his devotion to problems of public welfare, a leader for many years in every aspect of the public good. Mr. John Smith.

PRESENTING THE CITATION

Mr. Richard Stone, evidence of your philanthropies appears throughout this community. You helped build the Mercy Hospital and the Youth Center, and there are many other monuments of your devotion to the community. You have helped the present campaign with your usual zeal. It is my privilege on behalf of the Committee to present to you this illuminated and engraved citation which I will read:

> "The contribution he has made to the health, welfare, and well-being of his fellow citizens and the years of devoted service to civic and philanthropic causes have earned the gratitude of the community."

It is with deep pride that we pay this tribute to you —an outstanding leader and friend. Your interest and devotion to the welfare of your fellow-man has set a precedent of community responsibility, philanthropy, and brotherhood which serves as an inspiration for all of us. We, the members of the committee, are happy to have this opportunity to express publicly our high regard to a friend and colleague, and to show our admiration for your life and work.

ACKNOWLEDGING PRAISE AND CITATION

I am deeply grateful for the honor you have done me in presenting me with this beautiful citation. Life affords a man few joys more sweet than appreciation by his neighbors and colleagues. Your tributes and the award of this citation have moved me more than I can tell you. Let me add that I have done nothing more than to serve the community in my own humble way as best I could. I shall continue to serve as long as I am able. Thank you very much for everything.

10. Testimonial to a Public Official on Retirement

OPENING

There are few men in public life of whom it could be said with more feeling on the eve of their retirement: "Well done, thou good and faithful servant," than of

Senator Charles Jones. It is inspiring to know that politics can produce public servants such as he has proved himself to be. His long and distinguished career has added luster and distinction to the Senate. He has served his State extremely well. Senator Jones is one of the voices in the Senate that could always be counted upon to speak up for justice, for decency and for dignity. He has done much to humanize our laws and bring them into harmony with the economic conditions of this age. The Senate will sorely miss him. His unselfish devotion to public causes merits the tributes he will receive tonight.

INTRODUCING PRESENTOR OF GOLD CUP

A distinguished member of the community—our village mayor—has been asked to make a presentation to our guest of honor. It is my pleasure to introduce Mayor Samuel Smith.

PRESENTING GOLD CUP

Senator Jones' retirement provides a happy opportunity to pay tribute to him for his accomplishments and his many services to our State. Rare indeed is the man who can point to a quarter-century of selfless devotion to his fellow-man. His twenty-five years of service gives us all a chance to celebrate his deeds, reflect on his wise guidance, and toast his outspoken courage, steadfastness, and devotion.

His wealth of experience and knowledge, his large acquaintance and great popularity have made him an outstanding personality. His efforts on behalf of our State have contributed more than any other thing to its progress and welfare. As a token of our affection, the committee has recommended that we take some definite action to commemorate his retirement. We thought something to place in his home or office to remember the good-will of this organization would be appropriate. We are, therefore, presenting him with a gold cup as a measure of the esteem in which he is held. And I may add that if this cup were as big as this room all of the good wishes of our membership would fill it to overflowing. And so, on behalf of the community, I present to you, Senator Jones, this gold cup, which is engraved:

"Awarded to Senator Charles Jones for his distinguished service in advancing the health, education, and welfare of the people of his State."

THANKING SPEAKER

I am sure that our guest of honor will always recall with a glow of pride and satisfaction the tribute paid to him by Mayor Smith and the presentation of the gold cup.

INTRODUCING PUBLIC OFFICIAL

It is with pleasure that I present the great Governor of our great State. He needs no words of introduction or praise from me. The effectiveness of his administration is the highest commendation that he can receive. Governor Steven Stone.

ADDRESS OF TRIBUTE

I am pleased indeed to join in the tributes to Senator Charles Jones and to extend to him my heartiest best wishes on the occasion of his retirement from official life. Although I have known for some time that for personal reasons he would not continue his services to the Senate, I am indeed sorry that he now finds it necessary to return to private life. However, now that he has made his decision I am glad to salute his contributions and wish him well.

Senator Jones, you retire to private life with the satisfaction of knowing that you have made a substantial contribution to your community and the State.

Public service not infrequently demands of those who seek its rewards the possession of many good qualities and virtues. None of your colleagues will forget your wise counsel and calm confidence in the face of every kind of difficulty—your concern for the welfare of the people—the warm heart as well as the skill you brought to every job. You have carried a heavy burden of responsibilities in a job where brickbats usually outnumber thanks. But it is only necessary to remember the number of good laws on the statute books which you authored to know that you deserve a big hand for work well done. You have never considered your personal comfort or interests when it was necessary to correct an evil condition. No man could more readily than you understand the range of a problem and go right to the core.

It is my distinct pleasure to salute you, Senator, and wish you good health, good luck, and the best of everything.

THANKING SPEAKER

Thank you, Governor Stone, for taking time out of a

very busy schedule to come here to pay tribute to our guest of honor. We, in the community, can rejoice that Senator Jones' wise counsel, experience and courage will be still available to us. When we appeal to him for assistance, as we are bound to do, it will be a comfort to know that his talents will be at our disposal.

INTRODUCING GUEST OF HONOR

Without further ado, I present our guest of honor who I know will want to respond to the things that have been said about him. Senator Charles Jones.

RESPONSE BY GUEST OF HONOR

I am quite overwhelmed. I find it hard to express my gratitude. First, I must acknowledge the very generous and lavish praise and thank you for your display of affection and friendship. I am particularly happy so many of you could come. I am deeply moved and complimented by your gift of a gold cup commemorating my retirement from public life. Truly, my cup of happiness runneth over. No gift could be more appreciated nor give me greater joy. I thank the Governor for his presence here and for his fine tribute and I would like him to know that it was an honor to have served with a man who is so devoted to the people of the State. To Mayor Smith, my sincerest thanks for all that he has so extravagantly said about my accomplishments and to Fred Fund for the excellent way he presided at this wonderful dinner and to each of you for the courtesy you have shown me by coming here tonight that I might greet you. Above all, I should pay a salute to my wife, Jane, for all she did to make my political career possible—for her fortitude, her faith, her magnificent courage, her insistence on simplicity in all things—my debt to her is very great. It only remains that I should say, not goodbye—I do not want to say that—but goodnight, and God bless you.

CLOSING

Senator, you well deserve the words of praise and appreciation voiced here tonight. I predict for you the same success in private life that you have enjoyed in your many years of distinguished public service. We are happy that you will continue your activities in the community and that we will frequently see you here. God bless you and aid all your endeavors.

11. Physician-of-the-year Award

OPENING

We have been brought together to honor a benefactor of the community. Our guest of honor came to this community thirty years ago. His untiring industry, sound sense, and unswerving fidelity soon attracted attention and he rapidly acquired a large practice. Whoever sought his services and followed his advice did not fail to profit from it. His success is the result of inherent strength of character and intelligent application. His zeal and devotion to his community have never failed or faltered. Whenever an individual or social service organization needed help, our guest of honor could always be counted on to provide it.

It is a wonderful privilege for us to see Dr. Robert Bookman publicly rewarded—to see his qualities publicly appreciated.

INTRODUCING LAWYER

The legal counterpart of our guest of honor, who is his life-long friend, has come here to pay tribute to him. Like our guest of honor, his roots are deep in his community. He too serves on the school board, heads the charity drives, and is a man of action whenever the community needs leadership. It is my honor to present Mr. Richard Blackstone.

TRIBUTES

Our friend and physician, Dr. Robert Bookman, is a man of science, learning, and skill. His profound knowledge and experience have won for him widespread recognition in his profession. Like many men of accomplishment he is unaffected and unassuming. By his integrity and great learning he has earned for himself a place of great distinction in the community.

During his long and very active career, Dr. Bookman has been called upon by his fellow-citizens to take a prominent part in many civic movements. His position as a leader among physicians is recognized by the members of his profession in the area and, undoubtedly, the community regards him as a great doctor.

Dr. Bookman is known for his unfailing courtesy to everyone. Every patient who enters his office finds in him a friend and an inspiration. This sketch would not be complete without referring to his charitable disposition. He is connected with every community enterprise which has for its object the alleviation of suffering and the relief of the needy and the afflicted. Together with Mrs. Bookman he helped to establish and support the Home of the Aged. He is a subscriber to many other charitable organizations. To his task of repairing sick bodies he brings not only a sound medical background but an unquenchable enthusiasm and an affection for his patients which obviously help in their recovery. His sense of humor is also on tap for those who are tense and worried. It is very proper that a man who does so much to maintain the honor and dignity of the medical profession should receive the public appreciation of the community and the designation "Physician-of-the-Year."

INTRODUCING SPEAKER FOR PRESENTATION

The person who has been chosen to make a presentation to our guest of honor is active in all things benefiting humanity. His theory of life is that he is going to pass this way but once and if, in passing, he can add any pleasure to the lives of those he met, he would do it, and he is doing it. He loves people and people love him. I present with pleasure, a friend of our guest of honor, Mr. William Church.

PRESENTING HONORARY MEMBERSHIP CARD

I have a very pleasant duty to perform and that is to present to Dr. Robert Bookman a tangible reminder of the affection we have for him. We would like Dr. Bookman to honor us as we would honor him. We would like him to become one of us in this organization.

What I say of Bob is not hearsay but from a close friendship with him for more than twenty years. He is a man who is devoted to his family, his profession, his community. He is an able, painstaking and conscientious doctor. Nothing can turn him aside from the path he has marked for himself. He has no desire for ease or the accumulation of great wealth. Bob has taken an active part in every community welfare program and has aided every fund-raising drive. He impresses everyone with his physical and mental vigor and energy. Dr. Bookman is a man of vitality and imagination who has attained eminence in his profession and community. It is, therefore, my privilege to present to him this gold honorary membership card which is inscribed:

"Presented to Dr. Robert Bookman, Physician-of-the-Year, in grateful appreciation for all he has done for the needy and afflicted. The call of duty has never gone unanswered. To his patients he gives his best efforts, the benefit of his wide knowledge, large experience, and untiring diligence."

This community owes Dr. Bookman a great debt. In a small way a doctor shares the lives of a great many people.

He knows their troubles, worries with them, does his best to make them well and happy, and is glad with them when he succeeds. A good doctor is, within the limits of his own field, the servant of the humblest individual who needs his services. Dr. Bookman has been many things to the members of our community and we are grateful.

I hope that in the years to come he will enjoy good health and happiness.

ACCEPTING HONOR

It would be quite unnatural if I were not deeply touched by this evidence of your good-will. I am proud to be the recipient of this gold membership card and I accept it with gratitude and a deep sense of humility. It is because this gift from you implies that I am considered worthy that I will treasure and hold it dearly.

I have really done nothing more than in my own humble way to serve this fine community as best I could. I shall continue to serve as long as I am able. Any doctor who is even moderately active sees in the course of a year a good many patients. In my years of practice, I have had many people tell me of their sicknesses, anxieties and problems. From this store of experience I have learned that every man, woman, and child, regardless of his station in life, regardless of racial origin, is worthy of and should be treated with respect, as befits the essential dignity of man.

I want to thank my friend Bill Church for his fine presentation and Dick Blackstone for his very generous tributes and our chairman for his excellent conduct of the meeting. I cannot tell you the pleasure I feel in being an honorary member of this great Association. The work of the Association is such as to deserve real commendation for its efforts in building a better community.

CLOSING

Doc Bookman is a most useful citizen and a great friend of the sick. We hope he will be with us for many years to come.

We conclude with the delivery by Reverend Lake of the well-known and inspiring prayer by Charles Lewis Slattery.

CLOSING PRAYER

"Almighty God, we thank Thee for the job of this day; may we find gladness in all its toil and difficulty, in its pleasure and success, and even in its failure and sorrow. We would look always away from ourselves, and behold the glory and the need of the world that we may have the will and the strength to bring the gift of gladness to others; that with them, we may stand to bear the burden and heat of the day and offer Thee the praise of work well done. Amen."

12. Presentation of Scientific Award

Dr. Samuel Shield without fanfare or publicity has spent twenty years of his brilliant medical career on the staff of Hope Hospital. Because of the medical staff's high regard for his outstanding service in the public interest, he is being fittingly honored tonight. One of the tributes paid to him by his medical colleagues and personal friends takes the form of the establishment of a fund in his name to memorialize his scientific contribution. Despite great gains in medicine in recent years, the country faces many health problems. Because of these great strides and the consequent increase in life expectancy, one of the most serious problems will be the care of persons with chronic diseases. The fund will be used to establish and maintain the "Dr. Samuel Shield Medical Library" at the Hope Hospital. Any gifts to the Dr. Shield Library will be most welcome. All money will be used to provide for the purchase of books and the enlargement of the library.

INTRODUCING COLLEAGUE

I have the honor of introducing an intimate friend

and associate of our guest of honor. He is loved and respected by everyone who knows him. Dr. Richard Hart.

TRIBUTES TO SCIENTIST

Having worked closely with Dr. Shield during his many years at Hope Hospital, I know the value of his accomplishments on behalf of humanity. It is fitting that these tributes be paid to him. "Doc" Shield is a rare human being. Whatever he touches, he brightens. His warmth of personality is boundless. It has been his custom to be with his patients on holidays or after special occasions to help them "celebrate" instead of taking the day off. This and many other personal considerations shown to the sick under his care endeared him to all, helped them in time of need, and comforted them in final sorrow.

I have worked closely with Dr. Shield for the past twenty years, and I know the value of his accomplishments on behalf of humanity.

No one has ever heard him complain. As we go through this busy life sometimes callous to the feelings of others, it is remarkable to meet an individual so considerate, so kind, so self-effacing as is Doc Shield.

Every year this great man is with us, the world is a better place in which to live. He is regarded as a friend of everyone in this community. He is a great and deservedly well-loved citizen of the community.

Dr. Shield has given his time to many good causes. He brings to the problems of community health the knowledge and long experience of a family physician. In honoring him, Communities Association honors itself.

It is my privilege to present to him this citation, which I will read:

> "Because of Dr. Samuel Shield's leadership in the community and his great contribution to human welfare in the field of medical research particularly and to the community health generally, he merits this citation.
>
> "The work of Dr. Shield is in the highest tradition of selfless and dedicated medical research. He has provided the knowledge and means for the control of a dread disease. By helping scientists with technical information, by offering them the benefit of his years of experimentation and research and by welcoming them to his laboratory that they may gain fuller knowledge, Dr. Shield has done much to advance scientific knowledge."

May you have a long, long life, so that we may add another jewel to the crown of our scientific world of great men.

RESPONSE TO SPEAKER

Thank you, Dr. Hart. Those who worked with and for Dr. Shield have the same admiration for him, not only for his keen and questioning mind but for the personal traits that made him a friend and mentor to so many on his staff.

INTRODUCING GUEST OF HONOR

This is a worthy public acknowledgment of an unusual civic leader. The people of this community have often recognized the value of Dr. Shield's contribution by calling on him to serve in many advisory capacities. But this is the first time he has received the public homage of his neighbors.

I am pleased to call upon our guest of honor, Dr. Samuel Shield.

ACCEPTANCE OF AWARD

I am deeply indebted for the compliments paid to me. I am indebted to the Communities Association for sponsoring this meeting. The good work of the Association is well known. The way our democracy is geared, especially at the municipal level, it is important that an enlightened and interested group should take a deep interest in the social welfare of the community.

Many thanks to my colleagues at the Hospital, as well as to the community, for giving me and my staff an opportunity to devote ourselves to arthritis research with "peace of mind." While no cure has resulted from our efforts, important facts have been discovered which at least will help control the crippling disease. We may have the opportunity to see, in our lifetime, the beginning of the end of the fear of this malady and other fears that plague mankind.

I am sure you know how I feel when you single me out for the warm and generous sentiments you have just expressed and for this citation. Nothing remains for me but to thank you from the bottom of my heart, not only for the honor which has been conferred, but for your kindness.

My friends, I conclude with a pledge: With whatever talents the good God has given me, with whatever strength there is within me, I will continue my work to control or conquer this crippling disease which afflicts so many.

CLOSING

A great opportunity is open to the community today—an opportunity to contribute to man's ultimate victory over one of his greatest scourges. The struggle to achieve that victory has been well named a crusade, for only with faith and zeal and courage will the war against arthritis eventually be won. The first requisite to win it is adequate financial support for research and education. I am confident that this community will contribute with heartening generosity.

One of the outstanding contributions made to Hope Hospital by Dr. Shield was the establishment, ten years ago, of the Arthritis Clinic made possible by the generous gift of a grateful patient. In the field of arthritis research, Dr. Shield has developed important scientific data. He has carried on an extensive program of teaching at Hope Hospital as well as in medical schools.

Dr. Shield's achievement is service of the highest magnitude for the community, the nation, and mankind. We all recognize our debt of gratitude to him and his staff.

13. A Brotherhood Award

I extend to you a sincere welcome on the occasion of the presentation of the Brotherhood Award to Chester Snow. Each year we award to a worthy individual a citation for effective work in advancing good-will among the groups that comprise America. We regard these annual presentations as an occasion for planning for the future rather than a reason for tabulating past successes and accomplishments. Not that we intend to ignore them, but what lies ahead is challenging and provocative. I am confident that all of you will help to make the coming years an era of solid progress.

Chester Snow, whom we honor today, has a genuine love for human beings. He has been active in stimulating educational programs for justice, amity, understanding and cooperation among all peoples. He has done much to alleviate and, where possible, eliminate the prejudices which disfigure and distort business, social, and political relationships among our citizens. He is truly a good citizen. He has our esteem, respect, and affection.

INTRODUCING SPEAKER

Our speaker is endowed with courage, vision, ability, and a profound faith in humanity. His compassion, his understanding, his love, embraces all mankind, regardless of sect, creed, or race. We need such men to build a better world—a world of peace and human brotherhood and understanding among peoples. It is my privilege to introduce to you, Dr. Freeman Frank.

PRESENTING SCROLL

I can only heavily underscore what the toastmaster has said about Chester Snow. I speak as a member of the community who is fortunate to enjoy his friendship and companionship. He has made a tremendous contribution to the welfare of this community. There are few who show a more sympathetic love of their fellow-men. His interest in public affairs is great. One of Mr. Snow's achievements—in which he takes special pride—is the establishment in the community of a Conference of the various religious faiths designed to stimulate understanding. He has promoted an educational program for understanding and cooperation among the religious groups that comprise the community and has fortified efforts for a better world for all men.

It is entirely fitting that this scroll be awarded to a man whose distinguished career stands as a shining example for all to follow. It is, therefore, my privilege to present to you, Chester Snow, this citation which reads:

"For more than ten years, Chester Snow gave,
to the movement to encourage good-will among

American racial and religious groups, leadership, encouragement and inspiration. The fight for civil rights is never-ending, and has seldom demanded more courage and steadfastness than during the years when Mr. Snow headed the Committee for Promotion of Brotherhood. Those high traits he possesses in full measure.

"With insight into the needs of democracy, with unfaltering opposition to those who would render us less free and with gentleness and warm friendship toward his co-workers, Chester Snow has led the campaign efficiently and valiantly.

"With abiding gratitude and affection we tender him this memento of years of treasured association."

The breadth of your service to the community, Chester, has indeed been outstanding. You should have a sense of great satisfaction in the splendid contribution you have made to the advancement of human values. You have effectively assisted in increasing good-will and cooperation among all peoples and groups. Your great abilities have been devoted to a high purpose. You are helping to keep alive in the heart of humanity the bright hope that freedom will some day supplant tyranny and oppression.

INTRODUCING GUEST OF HONOR

I now give the audience the real gift of the occasion, Mr. Chester Snow. He has performed great things for the community, without fanfare and often without public recognition. I present, with considerable pleasure, Mr. Chester Snow.

ACCEPTING TRIBUTES

I appreciate the attendance here this evening of so many of my friends. The demonstration of your affection is in itself compensation for my years of community service. To all, my heart goes out in thankfulness for your kind words and generous tributes. I thank God for the bounties I have received, for the wonderful friends I have and the fine family that He has given me. Finally, may He give me a wise and understanding heart so that when the final chapter is ended and the Book is closed, history may record my devotion to the cause of the Brotherhood of man under the Fatherhood of God.

I am singularly rich in friendships. Friends of all ages have contributed enormously to my happiness and helped me greatly in times of need. I learned one of the great secrets of friendship early in life—to regard each person with whom one associates as an end in himself, not a means to one's own ends.

Edwin Markham wrote:

"There is destiny that makes us brothers,
None goes by his way alone,
All that we send into the lives of others,
Comes back into our own."

I very much appreciate all that has been said. Thank you very, very much for coming here.

CLOSING

Every now and then a leader arises in the community who attains distinction because of his qualities of mind and character. Such a person is Chester Snow—a vigorous champion of justice and equality for all.

It is my fervent wish that the honor and happiness which Chester and his family are now enjoying may continue and increase for the rest of their days.

I will close by reciting the legend etched on the base of the Statue of Liberty in New York harbor:

"Give me your tired, your poor,
Your huddled masses yearning to breathe free,
The wretched refuse of your teeming shore.
Send these, the homeless, tempest-tossed to me:
I lift my lamp beside the golden door."

14. A Garden Club Meeting

WELCOME

On behalf of the Garden Club we bid you welcome. We hope you will enjoy the program we have arranged for you and that when you return to your homes it will be with pleasant recollections of a few well-spent hours with your neighbors. I now call upon our Program Chairman, Mrs. George Goode.

INTRODUCING HORTICULTURIST

I know you have been looking forward in pleasant anticipation to meeting our guest speaker. He is a well-liked member of the community and is widely respected for his knowledge of horticulture. The subject of his talk is one on which he is exceptionally qualified to speak with both wisdom and authority. He is regional director of the National Landscape Association and past president of the Horticultural Foundation. In connection with his work as landscape architect, he has been called upon to establish gardens hundreds of miles from home. He has lectured on the platform, on radio and television. His subject is garden planting and garden maintenance. I have the pleasure to present the man who is responsible for much of the good landscaping in our community, Mr. Allen Dale.

ADDRESS ON SUBJECT OF GARDENING

A popular textbook on gardening opens with the advice that to have a good garden, hire a good gardener. This advice is sound but you, too, can learn to become a good gardener. In the last few years there has been an enormous increase in the number of amateur gardens. Gardening provides the gardener with an opportunity for self-expression. In these tense and busy days some such hobby becomes a necessity. It fills the need for self-expression and is pleasant exercise in the open air. The garden is never crowded and there is no waiting to tee off—and you don't have to travel to get to it.

I will now show you some slides illustrating proper garden planting and maintenance. (*The slides are projected and he explains them.*)

ANNOUNCING QUESTION PERIOD

Mr. Dale realizes only too well how many are the problems that beset the beginner in gardening. He has answered literally thousands of questions put to him by amateurs and experienced gardeners and I am sure he will be glad to answer yours. (*Questions and answers follow.*)

THANKING SPEAKER

The audience has indicated in a most impressive manner their appreciation of Mr. Dale's talk. I am sure he has helped to stimulate in many of us a love for gardening. We offer our thanks to him for his help and advice. We thank him also for that friendliness of manner which has given so much warmth to every moment of his presence with us.

THANKING PROGRAM CHAIRMAN

I cannot let this opportunity pass without expressing the appreciation of the Garden Club for the active, intelligent and hard work which has been done by the chairman of the program committee, Mrs. George Goode. She not only arranged the program, and the refreshments which follow, but canvassed the members by telephone to make sure they would attend.

We have now come to the end of the program. Our Program Chairman has provided us with an enjoyable afternoon. The speaker has been interesting and delightful. You have shown appreciation by your applause in a very eloquent way. If there is no objection, the meeting stands adjourned.

15. Town Hall Meeting

OPENING

We welcome you to the annual open meeting of the Town of Centerville. Town Hall meetings are an important institution in our way of life. Freedom of discussion and exchange of ideas—those things we value—were born of such meetings.

Tonight we will have nominations for the election of two town trustees. We will hear the annual report of the Mayor followed by open discussion and there will be an opportunity to express our views and ideas for the betterment of the community. At the conclusion of the meeting refreshments await you.

NOMINATIONS

The Chairman of the Nominating Committee, Mr. Sam Brown, will please make his report of nominations for the office of Town Trustee, to serve for two years. (*Report is made.*)

You have heard the report of the nominating committee. Are there any further nominations? A motion having been made and seconded to close nominations, if there is no objection nominations will be closed. Those in favor of the slate say "Aye," opposed, "Nay." The slate is declared unanimously nominated.

INTRODUCING MAYOR

Our Mayor heads an organization that employs twenty full-time persons, and levied taxes of $100,000 last year on property assessed at one million dollars. Centerville's financial condition is so good we are considered one of the best municipal risks in the State. Such an operation calls for great executive ability, which our Mayor has in good measure. He does his job without fanfare and gives it the benefit of his wide experience and knowledge. He has given many years of his life to the service of good government and the honest administration of his office. With pride I present Mayor Spear who will give his Annual Report which will be followed by open discussion (*Annual Report is delivered.*)

QUESTION AND ANSWER PERIOD

The Mayor will be pleased to answer any question concerning town affairs. If I may, to break the ice, I will ask the first question: "Is there any plan afoot to replace the village hall with a more modern building?" (*Discussion follows.*)

THANKING MAYOR

Every now and then a leader arises in a community who attains an enviable reputation for devotion to public service. Such a person is our Mayor Spear.

CLOSING

This concludes our meeting. Your active interest and participation in town affairs is very important to its welfare. Thank you for coming. Please stay for the refreshments.

16. Dedicating a Home for the Aged

OPENING

The Reverend Paul Paulson will invoke the Divine Blessing.

DIVINE BLESSING

Almighty God, we beseech Thee, for all who are devoted to the betterment of humanity, broaden our horizons so that we may see that the goal of life is greater than bread and meat, and help us realize that all men are our brothers. Hasten the day of peace and concord in world affairs, we pray Thee, and grant us peace and happiness for all generations.

WELCOME

I appreciate the privilege of presiding at these ceremonies. The opening of the Home for the Aged has been a goal for which we have worked, planned, and sacrificed. All of us should applaud the committee, the many workers and contributors, for this dream-come-true. The community has made a good beginning toward recognizing its responsibility to the elderly citizens. It is a monument to those who have envisioned it. The Home we now dedicate will be staffed by personnel trained in geriatric problems. The Home for the Aged will render service on the basis of human dignity and individual worth. No guest will ever pay a cent for his care.

INTRODUCING COMMITTEE CHAIRMAN

The Chairman of the Building Committee has served with energy and effectiveness and with the same zeal that he has shown in all other positions he has undertaken. His love for this edifice is so strong that all his waking moments have been spent hastening the day when its facilities would be made available to those who need them. I present the Chairman of the Building Committee, Mr. Fulton Fund.

DEDICATORY ADDRESS

I appreciate the honor of being chosen to take part in the dedication of this fine Home. I am sure that everyone here is impressed by its beautiful setting and sturdy construction..

The test of the conscience of a community is in its attitude toward its aged, its distressed and its sick. Today that test is being met intelligently.

We are here to dedicate this new Home. In one sense we cannot dedicate a building to anything. It remains stone. In reality we are here to re-dedicate ourselves as members of the community. This building is but a symbol—the outward manifestation of an idea and an ideal. The Home we are dedicating memorializes our responsibility to the community.

The care of our aging is our obligation. The obligation applies to us individually and collectively. Our elders must be kept healthy and happy. It is not only a real joy to be able to take care of those who cared for us and brought us to this time of our lives, but it is our responsibility.

We publicly express sincere thanks to the great many people who aided in bringing about the completion of this great work. We are grateful to the civic, religious, and social groups which helped in this project—to the many men and women of the community who by their contributions made possible this magnificent event. The community owes a special debt of gratitude to the men and women who envisioned this Home for the Aged. It is fitting to dedicate this structure to them in grateful acknowledgment of a debt for which there can be no repayment.

I felt signally honored when the presiding officer invited me to help dedicate the edifice. But my pleasure was immeasurably increased when I was asked to make a presentation of the building key to Mr. Roy Rankin, the President of the Board of Directors of the Home for the Aged.

PRESENTING BUILDING KEY

This key which opens the door to a much-needed refuge for our senior citizens has little intrinsic value. It is merely a symbol. After you have received it, Mr. Rankin, you will, no doubt, put it away never to use again. The doors of this beautiful structure will always be open to all aged and needy applicants of the community regardless of race or creed. The door will not be closed to any of them. I now present this key to you with the knowledge that it opens the door to the best care modern science can devise and the generosity of the members of the community can afford.

ACCEPTING BUILDING KEY

On behalf of the Home for the Aged and its Board of Directors, I acknowledge and accept this key to the Home building. I accept it with a deep sense of responsibility. This new building can be no more than a prologue. We have built only a doorway, and our obligation today is to look forward through it. This Home is an expression of faith in private initiative in the field of human welfare.

I am confident that a grateful community will find means to maintain this splendid institution. Whether we can open the doors even wider will depend upon their generosity. Certainly, we take pride in the fulfillment of our determination to have a Home for the Aged as fine as this we are dedicating. The Home we are dedicating provides the elderly with recreation and activity facilities which will give them a feeling of usefulness and belonging, of adequacy and accomplishment. It is worthy of the support of the community. We are fully cognizant of the unselfishness of the civic, religious, and labor organizations in meeting the physical, emotional, and spiritual needs of the aging who will spend their sunset years in the Home. This is indeed a public service and a humanitarian contribution to our society. The Home memorializes the community's responsibility to the aging.

It is fitting to dedicate this structure to our civic, religious, and labor organizations in grateful acknowledgment for their work.

CONSECRATION PRAYER

Almighty and everlasting God, who governs all things in heaven and earth, mercifully hear the supplications of Thy people, and grant us peace all the days of our life. Most heartily we beseech Thee, to behold and bless our aged and ailing and so replenish them with the grace of Thy Holy Spirit that they may always incline to Thy will and walk in Thy way. Endow them plenteously with heavenly gifts; grant them in health and happiness long to live. Almighty God, graciously enable us now to dedicate this house which we have erected to the honor and glory of Thy name, and be mercifully pleased to accept this service at our hands. Amen!

In the name of the community which envisioned this project, we do solemnly dedicate this Home.

CLOSING

What was considered by many as a dream has now become a reality. This fine building is a tribute to the foresight, planning, and cooperation of the members of the community. Today, we make good a promise to the community and to ourselves.

The problem of our aging keeps mounting as the life span increases. We are determined to give them a Home and the best care that modern medical knowledge can devise. We assumed that obligation as members of the community.

However, this is just the beginning. Our obligation is a continuing one. The Home must be properly maintained. Older persons are more apt to be disabled and succumb to illnesses. When sick or disabled, they require help for longer periods. The need for hospitalization is greater.

The great debt which society owes to them for all their years of service, we are helping to repay in this very fine way.

17. Dedicating a Recreation Center

We have gathered today for an important occasion. The dedication of the Recreation Center has great significance for our community. It is a great pleasure to welcome you to these dedication ceremonies. Bishop Ernest Land has graciously consented to deliver the opening prayer.

INVOCATION

Almighty and Everlasting God, vouchsafe we beseech Thee to direct, sanctify and govern both our hearts and bodies in the ways of Thy laws and in the works of Thy commandments that through Thy most merciful being we may be preserved in body and soul. Direct us, O Lord, in all our doings with Thy most gracious favor that in all our works begun, continued and ended in Thee, we may glorify Thy holy name, and finally, by Thy mercy obtain everlasting life. Amen!

INTRODUCING SPEAKER

Our speaker is interested in problems of our youth. His philosophy of government and his approach to civic problems are notable for their humanitarianism. He has led the fight for such objectives as more parks, better schools, improved child-care programs, good housing and social cooperation. He is a symbol of the intelligent, informed, and independent legislator. With profound satisfaction, I present Congressman Frank Smith.

DEDICATORY ADDRESS

This marks a significant step in the fulfillment of a hope. This organization may indeed be proud of the role it has taken for the betterment of the community. It has made a real contribution to the solution of a current problem. It should be stressed from the beginning that the work being done is preventive, not corrective. The youngsters to be served are good boys from good families. They deserve every opportunity to remain so. Recreation centers give boys that chance. They provide wholesome fun for their leisure time, healthful outlets for their excess energy, proper instruction and the opportunity to play at competitive sports, to acquire useful hobbies and to learn skills and handicrafts. They provide playgrounds, ballfields, and club houses.

Great effort and thought, as well as much money, have gone into the erection of this Recreation Center. Your contributions will add immeasurably to the happiness of neighborhood youngsters and the well-being of our entire community. The success of the enterprise is dependent upon continuous, dedicated, and highly skilled effort.

It is my solemn privilege to dedicate this edifice which is a silent memorial of our responsibility to the community. What the destiny of this structure shall be is in our hands.

May the Supreme Architect of the Universe guide us and give us divine assistance in lifting our hearts, our souls, to greater heights for the welfare of all His children!

THANKING SPEAKER

We owe much to Congressman Smith's unflagging interest and support of our community affairs. This Recreation Center, which he has so impressively dedicated, is only one of the many causes he sponsors. The community is proud of you, Congressman.

CLOSING

This is a big day for the entire community, especially for the workers who toiled to bring this dream to realization. It is only a beginning, but a proud one. The community has a challenging opportunity for service in the years ahead. You have shown that you are ready to meet the challenge.

This Center should repay its costs many times over in building good citizens. It is a doorway through which a growing child can be made aware that here there is understanding, sympathy, and a friendly interest.

The dedication of our Recreation Center represents a great opportunity for members of our community to render service. It has taken bold and courageous planning to bring to its fruition this magnificent Recreation Center. It has been worth it. To say that we have reached our goal would be misleading, but the summit is in sight. It is hoped that the community will continue its efforts on behalf of this great humanitarian project. What remains to be done is to make funds available for several years of unbroken maintenance of the Recreation Center. The campaign is continuing and the work to be done is just as important and necessary as that just completed.

The work of the members of the Building Committee cannot be compensated fully by words of praise. I, as chairman, can only say that without them the task would have been impossible.

18. The Cornerstone Dedication

OPENING

We have convened to lay the foundation stones of the Youth Center. The edifice to rise on this site will be devoted to promoting character development, to citizenship training and physical and spiritual fitness of the youth of the area. The Center when completed will provide wholesome recreation and social opportunities for boys and girls.

It is the custom upon occasions like the present to deposit beneath the cornerstone certain items of significance of the period in which it was laid. The various articles here safely enclosed are copies of all local newspapers, several current magazines, and a brochure describing the edifice which is to be erected here. I now deposit these articles beneath the cornerstone.

DEDICATION PRAYER

Almighty God, by Whom all things are made, grant that whatever shall be builded on this stone may be to Thy glory and the honor of Thy great name.

PROCLAMATION

I now proclaim that this cornerstone has been laid.

INTRODUCING SPEAKER

The dedicatory address will be made by one who has worked hard and diligently in initiating this project. He can be counted on to see it through to completion—Mr. Frank Ball.

ADDRESS

The building of this Youth Center and its maintenance is an undertaking worth supporting. It is a useful and a fruitful work. It would be more humane and ultimately more economical to understand the causes of youths' defiance and then try to eradicate them. It is impossible to point to any quick cure. There are, however, at least several areas upon which thought and attention should be focused. Everything which restores to the young person the sense of belonging, of having responsibilities and being wanted, are steps in the right direction. Churches, social agencies, block-by-block groups—in short, the whole complex of community life—must pull together to let our young people know that we have a deep interest in them. The problem is great and touches our society at the heart. The work we are doing here goes to the "hard core" of the problem.

This building will be a monument to the sense of responsibility of the community. Here it will stand, we hope, a long, long time, saying to all citizens that we mean to work long and patiently for the benefit of our young people. The facilities will be used by the children of the neighborhood without charge and without distinction of color or creed. We are truly proud of the community spirit which has initiated a project so much needed.

The speed with which this Center is completed will depend largely on the flow of contributions from donors to provide $200,000 to make the new institution a reality. I know that the citizens of this community who initiated this splendid project will see it through to a speedy and successful completion. These ceremonies are promises that no youth will be denied his birthright of a good childhood.

PRESENTING TROWEL

I have been asked to perform a very pleasant duty before closing, and that is to present to Mayor Samuel Smith this silver trowel as a memento of this occasion. The inscription on the trowel commemorates this event and bears the names of all the civic, social, school, and religious organizations of the community sponsoring the Youth Center. The honor is rightfully his, for all he has done for the community and for this project. I am proud to have been designated as the one to present this to you, Mayor Smith.

CLOSING

We will conclude the ceremonies with a prayer by Reverend George Green.

May the Supreme Architect of the Universe guard and bless this place and prosper all the laudable works of those connected with it! May He protect the craftsmen employed in this work from every harm. May our country continue in peace and prosperity throughout all generations. Amen!

19. Memorial Services

OPENING

We have gathered here to pay our tribute of farewell to the distinguished and revered Henry Hart, our beloved and esteemed colleague. He was a courageous champion of justice and freedom. His faith in God was unswerving. His devotion to America was strong and impassioned. He was a many-sided citizen. This community particularly owes much to Henry Hart for his aggressive and devoted toil in behalf of cultural and civic welfare and for his interfaith philanthropies. He held many positions of trust, confidence, and honor. He was a man of rare personal attraction, of a genial, generous nature, and full of kindness.

PRAYER

Almighty Father, in sorrow and gratitude we would give

Thee thanks for all the contributions and achievements of this Thy servant, Henry Hart, to the life of our community. He was of noble spirit, possessed of humanitarian principles and with a compassionate understanding of the suffering. His high moral integrity, lofty ideals, broad sympathies and unselfish devotion to democratic principles won for him the love and affection of the community. He was saintly in character, liberal in spirit and vigorous in mind. He had a love of people and an immense respect for the worth and dignity of the individual. He was endowed with a fine mind. He was kind and generous, and his manners were stamped with the gentleness and honesty of his nature. His fidelity and loyalty to his friends was one of his greatest traits. In his death the community has lost one of its principal leaders.

INTRODUCING PUBLIC OFFICIAL

I present one of the honored gentlemen of this community. He has attained a position of prestige, respect, and influence in public life. This position was earned by a solid faith in three great bulwarks of our way of life—faith in God, faith in America, and faith in his fellowman. His name is held in admiration and respect. Senator Samuel Shield.

EULOGY

We have sustained a grievous loss with the passing of our beloved friend Henry Hart. It is difficult to assess our loss. The world we live in seems poorer and less hopeful without him. The death of Henry Hart is a heavy misfortune for us and our community.

It was my good fortune to know Henry Hart intimately. His personality radiated charm and sweetness. As we go through this busy life sometimes callous to the feelings of others—it is remarkable to meet a man like Henry Hart. I know that the impress he left upon me is a durable one. He was one of nature's noblemen. He touched nothing that he didn't brighten and better. I don't think there is any man who came in contact with him who didn't add to his own determination to be better and more sympathetic and generous to his fellow-man.

He distinguished himself by his dedication and contribution to the welfare of his community. His spirit of humanity, of devotion to the good of all, carried over into all fields of endeavor, including charitable and philanthropic activities. His passing leaves a void in our hearts and in the community that will be difficult to fill. I extend my personal sympathies to his bereaved wife and family.

ANNOUNCEMENT

The Secretary of the Association, of which Henry Hart was a former president, will read a resolution of sympathy.

RESOLUTION OF SYMPATHY

Whereas the passing of our former president Henry Hart instills in us a feeling of deep sorrow, and

Whereas the late Henry Hart distinguished himself by his sincere dedication and substantial contribution to the welfare of the community, be it

Resolved that we, the officers and members of the Association, deeply regret the passing of our former president Henry Hart and do hereby offer our sincere and heartfelt sympathy and condolence to his beloved wife and family.

It is further resolved that a copy of this resolution be sent to the family of the late Henry Hart.

CLOSING

The only thing I can say in concluding is to repeat the words of Philip James Bailey:

> "We live in deeds, not years; in thoughts, not
> breath;
> In feelings, not in figures on a dial,
> We should count time by heart-throbs.
> He most lives who thinks most, feels the noblest,
> acts the best."

By those standards, no life was fuller than Henry Hart's.

The Lord in His love hath given, the Lord in His own judgment hath taken away. Blessed be the name of God!

20. Thanksgiving Day Ceremonies

We welcome you to these Thanksgiving services. Similar services are being held throughout the country in compliance with the proclamation of the President of the United States.

With so many other weeks in the year devoted to commercial or charitable purposes, it is good to have a week set aside for giving thanks. Thanksgiving is the time for enjoying the ritual of feast and family assembly. It is a time for counting our blessings and good fortunes and to reflect upon the many benefits and privileges which as a nation we enjoy. We, in our respective social service organizations, may wish to add thanks for the privilege of giving service—perhaps one of the greatest privileges of all. We should give thanks that ours is a land where people can laugh, and dream, and hope, and speak our minds and worship as we please. And we do have much to be thankful for. Almighty God has smiled on us and our beloved country.

INTRODUCING CLERGYMAN

Reverend Fulton Ford will deliver the invocation.

INVOCATION

Almighty God, our Heavenly Father, giver of all good gifts, we render thanks for Thy mercies and blessings, and ask Thy favor as we are here assembled. Guide us by Thy Spirit that in all our doings we may be enabled to glorify Thee. Guard and guide us through all our days. May reverence prevail, good will abound, and charity be practiced among us. We give thanks that our forefathers patterned a community to serve the spiritual and material needs of a diverse people. Mayest Thou bless our United States of America that it may ever safeguard the rights of life, liberty, and the pursuit of happiness. And in Thy good time may there come into our troubled world the assurance of universal harmony and peace. Amen.

INTRODUCING PUBLIC OFFICIAL

I have known few men with a greater sense of duty to their country, with a deeper sense of responsibility for its well-being and future than our next speaker whom I am proud to present, Senator Seymour Stand.

ADDRESS

We can mark Thanksgiving Day as it was meant to be marked with a sense of confidence and achievement.

The families that gather on this family holiday sense, as individuals, the glow of prosperity. They look about them upon a land blessed with abundance and fertility. They take account of an economic system that is moving forward under the impetus of full freedom. They sense the shifting currents of a world which, if it is still far from peace, seems at least ready to accept the idea that war is impossible.

When the authors of the Declaration of Independence made their pledge of freedom to the world, they dedicated all that they were and all that they had to the cause. They knew that those promises could be made good only in blood and suffering. As a people we may be called again in such trials; yet, not to be conscious of blessings is to be guilty of ingratitude.

This is the month of Thanksgiving to which many look forward. It is the Thank-You month to Almighty God, and the month in which we meditate and give thanks for the blessings that are ours. The custom of devoting one day each year is a wise one. It was first observed in the days before we became a nation. It is in keeping with our oldest traditions that at the fruitful season of the waning year we turn again to Almighty God in grateful acknowledgment of His manifold blessings.

At the time for thanksgiving, may we express our deep appreciation of those forbears who, more than three centuries ago, celebrated the first Thanksgiving Day. Through their industry and courage our nation was hewn from the virgin forest, and through their steadfastness and faith the ideals of liberty and justice have become our cherished inheritance.

May we lift up our hearts in gratitude for the abundance of our endowments, both material and spiritual, and for the preservation of our way of life. May we show our thanks for our own bounty by remembering those less fortunate, and may the spirit of the Thanksgiving season move us to share with them, giving aid to the ill and destitute. Let us observe this day with reverence. Let us bow before God and give Him humble thanks.

On this day let all of us, of whatever creed, foregather in our respective places of worship to give thanks to God. Let us give thanks for the Gettysburg Address and the Declaration of Independence and the Constitution and the Bill of Rights, for all the words of Americans engraved in marble on monuments and public buildings.

Let us give thanks that we are not a population of citizens waiting to do as we are told, but a nation by tradition and temperament of powerful dissenters. Let us give thanks that we have the right of free and open debate, a national unity and strength far greater than that of any nation which has tried to shackle the minds of its people. Let us give thanks for the dream each man carries privately in his heart and mind. And finally, let us give thanks that we live in the present—a time of turbulence and change and struggle and excitement—for the present is always more adventurous than the past.

THANKING SPEAKER

We appreciate the address made by Senator Seymour Stand. We are proud of his accomplishments as a lawmaker. He has the wisdom and the strength to move toward the objectives which he has outlined and to uphold the high principles which he has set forth.

CONCLUSION

We will conclude the ceremonies with the invocation by Reverend Fulton Ford.

INVOCATION

Almighty God, Thou Who hast drawn back the curtains of another night and revealed unto us the beauties of this day, we give Thee thanks. With grateful and humble hearts we come before Thee and we thank Thee for all the benefits we have received at Thy hands, for all Thy mercies of every kind. We bless Thee for the gift of life, for friendships, for duties, for high hopes, for precious opportunities, for doing good and right impulses.

Let us remember the Pilgrim Fathers who, fleeing from religious oppression, landed on a bleak, forbidding shore and began to carve out what became this great Republic which it is our happy destiny to love and serve. For their foresight, their courage, and their idealism, let us give thanks to the Power which has made and preserved us as a nation. Amen.

21. Veterans Day Observance

OPENING

The hour of eleven having arrived, it is fitting that we pause in meditation and silent prayer for our noble men who sacrificed their lives to maintain our highest traditions. This is a day when every American should give thanks to those who have done so much to make possible the way of life we cherish.

Let us bow our heads in silent prayer for everlasting peace! Let us pray that in our troubled world a road will be found to lasting peace—a kind that will go on and on! The battle will not be won until the whole wide world lives beneath a brilliant peaceful sun.

PRAYER

May the Lord permit His countenance to shine upon those who made the supreme sacrifice and upon this land and the ideals for which they gave their lives.

Let us give thanks for those who found this land, and shaped America, and made us what we are; for the men and women, living and dead, known and unknown, who have spoken the thoughts we shared, who have sung the songs we knew, who have built the things we dreamed.

MEMORIAL ADDRESS

This occasion is one of great national symbolism. It is dedicated to those men, living and dead, who served in all our wars. This day was set aside to honor all the veterans who have fought to keep the flag of freedom flying over this our cherished land.

On this day we renew our dedication to the eternal quest for the Holy Grail of lasting peace, not for ourselves alone, but for all mankind.

Let us pray for peace, but be prepared for war. We dedicate ourselves to be prepared to defend ourselves against aggression. We do not glorify war.

We meet here every year to express our debt to those who served; to express our pride in the valor of America's sons and daughters; to show our pride in the ideals for which they fought.

On this day we reaffirm the nation's obligation to all those who went into the Valley of the Shadow of Death. Our nation has never and must never neglect its obligation to honor those who died, to care for those who received lasting injury, are ill and destitute.

I now dedicate this monument to those who gave all they were and all they had to the cause of freedom. I will read the inscription etched on this monument:

> "In reverent recognition of the Divine Guidance and to the eternal memory of those who gave the last full measure of devotion to their country, this monument is dedicated humbly to their sacrifices in defense of our freedoms."

This monument will serve to keep alive and fresh and vigorous our appreciation of their greatness. We observe Veterans Day as one of remembrance.

CLOSING

Today will recall to many an unhappy recollection—Pearl Harbor Day—a day that will stand forever as the symbol of lack of vigilance, a dark reminder that our dereliction cost many young men their lives. Firmly, we resolve that this must never happen again. Never again must the enemy be permitted to catch us unguarded. This is a day, however, when we recall our debt to the war disabled—when we can resolve they must never be permitted to believe their sacrifices were in vain, or forgotten.

22. Flag Day Ceremonies

OPENING

Today is Flag Day. The President has called for general observance of this day. Under the protecting folds of this banner, generations of Americans have enjoyed the blessings of liberty and justice. It is fitting that as a nation, we pause and observe this day.

The civic and patriotic bodies of the community have been asked to lead suitable observances designed to remind all Americans of their priceless birthright as citizens living under the protection of the American Flag. The celebration has more meaning this year than ever before.

Federal, state, and local government buildings display the Flag on this day. Homes, too, can stand forth with a special luster if they carry the floating symbol of this country's old and continued search for the things that give worth and dignity to the human spirit.

We will begin the ceremonies with the Pledge of Allegiance, to be led by the Girl Scouts.

PLEDGE OF ALLEGIANCE

"I pledge allegiance to the Flag of the United States of America and to the Republic for which it stands, one Nation, under God, indivisible, with liberty and justice for all."

INTRODUCING MILITARY LEADER

General Thomas Tyler is a respected member of this community. He rose swiftly to the top during a military career spiced with deeds of daring. A major at the start of the last war, he was a major-general when it ended. A few years later he became a full general. I present General Thomas Tyler.

DEDICATING FLAGPOLE

I have been asked to unfurl the flag on the flagpole which one of the citizens of our community has donated. This Flag represents to him, as it does to us, freedom dearly won and deeply cherished, freedom that is worth living and fighting for.

On this day, let us be reminded that the American people must always be prepared to make every necessary sacrifice to safeguard American democracy and freedom.

We now unfurl the flag on the flagpole so generously donated by a proud citizen.

Flag Day is the day in our calendar devoted to the Star-Spangled Banner which is the symbol of a great people, the American people.

It is our remembrance of the past, and our hope for the future. It is the inspiration of our youth, the strength of our maturity and the comfort of old age.

It symbolizes the free press, the right to think and express our thoughts without fear. It guarantees religious freedom, the right to assemble, and a free vote. It is the emblem which can be freely saluted by our citizens regardless of their race, creed, and color.

All citizens should display Old Glory on Flag Day and all other patriotic holidays.

Your chairman has asked me also to explain the etiquette involved in displaying our Flag. It is easy to seem a little superior about such an act as hanging the Flag from homes. And it is always a temptation to say that there is small use in making such a gesture once a year; if one honors the Flag, honor should be given throughout the year. That is true, but it is only half true. The things one does on special occasions come to have a meaning of their own.

Some of us are struck by the apparent carelessness and ignorance of many onlookers as the American Flag passes by. May I call attention to the proper way to pay respect to the Flag as it passes in parade. Men not in uniform should remove their hats and place them at the left shoulder with the right hand over the heart. If they are not wearing hats they should stand at attention facing directly forward. Women not in uniform should place their right hand over the heart and stand at attention.

CLOSING

The American way is the way of civil liberties and constitutional government. We believe in these. We hold them dearer than our physical existence. To maintain and strengthen them we must now, as never before, organize our individual lives, our social and economic institutions, and prepare ourselves in these to give "the last full measure of devotion."

We deplore the evidences of a growing tendency on the part of Americans to take the blessings of America too much for granted and to "play down" the need for public recognition, respect, and devotion to such symbols of our dearly bought heritage as the Flag of the United States.

Let's all bring new glory to "Old Glory" by displaying it proudly on Flag Day.

23. The Hospital Fund Drive and Testimonial

OPENING

We have convened today to pay homage to Chester Jones who has done so much for Hope Hospital. And this is an opportunity to direct attention to the financial needs of the Hospital.

It is fitting that our guest of honor be lauded, because he has given to the cause of humanity years of selfless devotion. He is high-minded and public spirited. His many philanthropies entitle him to the lasting gratitude of his fellow-citizens.

INTRODUCING PRESENTOR OF AWARD

I present to you a devoted colleague of our guest of honor, the able and industrious chairman of the Board of Directors of Hope Hospital, who will make a presentation to Mr. Jones. Mr. Carl Carrol.

PRESENTATION

On behalf of the Board of Directors of Hope Hospital, I present this silver plaque to you, Chester Jones. It is inscribed:

> "To Chester Jones: In grateful recognition of your distinguished service in behalf of all people, your philanthropies to the community and, most especially, your devotion and achievements on behalf of Hope Hospital. We salute you on the occasion of the Testimonial Banquet tendered in your honor by the Board of Directors of Hope Hospital."

The names of the members of the Board appear at the end of the inscription. This presentation reflects a long established custom of presenting silver objects to individuals for outstanding services or deeds. The intrinsic value of this silver plaque is not great. Our desire is that you have some token of our regard and also a reflection in some measure, at least, of all the good work you have done. Please accept this gift with our sincere gratitude. Your loyalty, your tireless efforts and lasting contributions to Hope Hospital well merit this recognition. It is our hope that you may long enjoy health and happiness. May good fortune always be with you!

INTRODUCING PRESENTER OF GIFT

Our next speaker is one of the honored gentlemen of this community, and a member of the State legislature. He has held many important positions of trust and continues to hold public office. He has given many years of his life to the service of good government and to the honest administration of his office. He has come to make a presentation to our guest of honor on behalf of Hope Hospital. Senator Samuel Shield.

PRESENTING CHECK

I was very happy to be asked to say a few words of greeting to our guest of honor. We are all delighted that we have this opportunity to pay tribute to you, Chester Jones, in recognition of your activities on behalf of Hope Hospital and your contributions to the welfare and well-being of your fellow-citizens. You have the satisfaction of knowing that hundreds of persons have been restored to health and their lives made more fruitful because of your devotion. We have found you to be a wise and friendly counselor. In spite of the heavy pressure of business matters, you always seem to find time for any task, however difficult, that benefits the community.

The dinner committee, consisting of John Jones and Mary Brown, have handed to me a check for $50,000 payable to the order of Hope Hospital, the proceeds of this excellent event, to promote and continue the work of Hope

Hospital. It is my honor to turn this check over to you.

May I add that you well deserve the signal recognition you are receiving tonight.

INTRODUCING HOSPITAL OFFICIAL

I now call upon the director of research and laboratories at the Hope Hospital who is performing a great service not only to the Hospital but to the community—Dr. Gilbert Gray.

TRIBUTE TO GUEST OF HONOR AND APPEAL FOR FUNDS

It is a privilege to have a part in these ceremonies honoring you. You have been the guiding force behind the Hospital campaign. I know it may become wearying to listen to enumerations of your services to the community, Chester, so I shall not inflict more on you than the occasion demands. I shall emphasize rather the need for every member of the community to help raise the money to sustain the work of the Hospital. We need the help of every resident if we are to raise the $100,000 needed to run and expand our Hospital.

There can be no more worthy cause than providing the sick and needy with the necessary facilities for restoring them to health. To help insure a greater Hope Hospital, we are trying to raise the money by public subscription. Many individuals, families, business and professional firms already have contributed liberally to the fund. All who live or work in the area served by the Hospital are being asked to join their fellow-citizens in accepting a share of the responsibility for the project. The movement to enlarge and modernize Hope Hospital now in progress is of the utmost importance to those who live in this community. Additional facilities are vitally needed because of the great increase in population.

I am certain that you will derive a sense of satisfaction by participating in so worthy a cause. Public contributions only support our program of treating patients, carrying forward research, and training personnel. Please contribute whatever you can afford—your gift in any amount will be gratefully received by the Hospital.

INTRODUCING GUEST OF HONOR

The spotlight is now on our guest of honor. It is difficult for me to add to the plaudits accorded Chester Jones. In view of his efforts on behalf of the community for so many years, the praise is not out of place. Mr. Jones will be long remembered if he had only half or a quarter of his career on the record. But it is a satisfaction to believe, as well as to hope, that his work is not nearly done. We need his mature mind. We are lucky to have him. I present Chester Jones.

ACKNOWLEDGING APPRECIATION

This has been a great night for me and it has brought me much joy. The knowledge that what I have done for the Hospital and the community is appreciated gladdens me. I had never anticipated tributes as warm as these.

I am indeed very thankful to you. I cannot, however, bring these remarks to a close without publicly expressing my gratitude to the directors of Hope Hospital, the civic leaders and public officials assembled here. It is most encouraging and heartening to win the approval of this distinguished group.

I intend to show my appreciation to you for coming here tonight by bringing these remarks to an end. So, in partial compensation for your coming to attend this celebration, I will say only, Good-night! And many, many thanks for all the nice things you have said and the things you are going to do for Hope Hospital. And the good Lord willing, I hope to continue this work as long as my health and strength will permit.

CLOSING

When I think of Chester Jones' interest in the Hospital and all his other humanitarian endeavors I think of these famous lines:

"Not what we give, but what we share,
For the gift without the giver is bare;
Who gives himself and alms feeds three,
Himself, his hungering neighbor and me."

The Hope Hospital is where Chester Jones' heart is and the welfare of the sick and needy has always been paramount to him. The continued welfare of its patients requires more facilities, and I am confident that the people of the community will make this project their own. Contributions in support of this worthy cause may be sent to the Hospital. They will help heal the sick, safeguard the well. Every contribution will be, indeed, a forward-looking investment in community well-being.

24. The Mental Health Fund Drive

OPENING

The Mental Health Fund Drive is under way in our community. We desperately need funds and volunteers. It is my sincere hope that you will open your hearts as never before and give generously of your time and money. On all sides we see signs of an awakened interest in the grave problem of mental health. We have become aware that our thrift in research spending has been very costly in human misery. The greatest public health problem today is not heart disease, cancer, or any other ailments which have received widespread attention in recent years. The number one health problem is mental illness. Mental illness is among the dreaded afflictions of mankind.

INTRODUCING PUBLIC OFFICIAL

I present to you a public official who realizes the urgent need to set up an intelligent program for the mentally ill. He has done much in his official capacity as head of the Health Department to intensify research and to provide the sick and needy with the benefits of early treatment so vital to them. He is a civic-minded person with a wealth of common-sense and a big heart. Commissioner of Health—Frank Flood.

APPEAL FOR FUNDS AND VOLUNTEERS

It is a privilege and a duty to speak for the Mental Health Fund which cares for the mentally sick of all races. It is a privilege because in America each of us has the freedom to exercise his own will in the administration of his personal affairs—it is a duty because each of us must be ever mindful of his sacred obligation under the common Fatherhood of God to help care for the underprivileged. Freedom to give is one of our great freedoms, and with all my heart, I endorse this appeal for volunteers and funds to establish additional facilities which are so badly needed.

The urgent task of meeting the health and welfare needs of the community cannot be performed by the municipality and the welfare agencies alone. They have neither the funds nor the personnel to meet these demands. It requires the assistance of all citizens of the community. We require private as well as public welfare agencies and programs to take care of our most pressing burden—human need and distress. We cannot afford to have less private welfare. We need more of it. The Mental Health Fund is an investment in the future of America. It represents a duty that has to be met. It is heartbreaking to hear the appeals of persons who need help and not be able to heed them.

Almost daily we are forced to turn away from our hospitals many of the sick and afflicted for lack of necessary facilities. We must add new facilities to keep pace with the growing demands. The program of the Mental Health Fund includes enlargement of research, intensification of early treatment, establishment of psychiatric facilities in communities, stimulation of training of professional personnel, and the discovery of methods to prevent relapses. It is indeed well to minister to and look after our sick. However, one cannot overlook the extreme importance of doing everything in our power to eliminate the cause and thus reduce the suffering.

The doors of our hospitals should be open to everyone regardless of race, creed, or ability to pay. The project needs the support of all who can give, and all those who can give only a little can still have the sense of full participation in a great neighborhood undertaking.

THANKING SPEAKER

Every citizen of the community knows of Commissioner Flood's conscientious performance of the duties of his office and appreciates the many tasks he has assumed voluntarily.

CLOSING

This appeal for funds and volunteers affords an opportunity to contribute to man's ultimate victory over one of his greatest scourges. We have an opportunity to support the continuing campaign for mental health.

We can combat mental illness by furthering research, training personnel, and providing the mentally ill with hospitals and clinics. It is a community effort we should all assist.

25. The Boy Scout Fund Drive

This is the kick-off of the annual Boy Scout drive. We appreciate your coming for this breakfast get-together. We will complete our business as quickly as possible that you may all return to your work and professions. You will pardon me if I take advantage of my status as presiding officer to allude briefly to the problems of our youth. They are problems we cannot shrug off. We need your support in the curent drive for funds so that the benefits of Scouting may reach more and more boys. We believe that Scouting represents some of the things that are essentially American in character. The Boy Scout movement has a three-fold emphasis upon health—health of body, health of mind, and health and soul. We know that our campaign will receive your wholehearted support.

INTRODUCING PUBLIC OFFICIAL

Our speaker—the only one this morning—is widely known as a public official with a passion for public service. He has devoted himself selflessly to many worthy enterprises—crusading for better schools, slum clearance, elimination of racial prejudice and the preservation of civil rights. He has shown a remarkable facility for getting things done. I present our popular Mayor, Samuel Smith.

APPEAL FOR FUNDS

The growth of the Boy Scout movement assures the nation of the future supply of citizens prepared in body, mind, and character to serve it.

Not always are boys who have gone wrong the product of slums, poverty, and ignorance. Many come from "nice" neighborhoods and schools, good homes and well-educated parents. Some may share their elders' restlessness and uneasiness in the shaky times in which we live. But it is comforting to know that more boys and girls turn out to be decent, respectable citizens than turn out bad.

The Boy Scouts need the active support of all who are interested in boys. More troops are needed to accommodate the thousands of boys who would be Scouts if they had the opportunity. Scouting here needs $500,000 for the next year. Of this amount, $200,000 would go for operation and extension of existing programs and $300,000 for camp improvements. This money will help bring Scouting to thousands of boys who want to enroll as Scouts. It will pay for training courses for Scout leaders, each of whom voluntarily gives hundreds of hours a year to Scouting.

The healthy emphasis of the Boy Scouts on skill and self-reliance in the service of others is well known to the people of this community. Boy Scouting gives a boy healthful outdoor adventure, knowledge and skills and a genuine understanding of fellowship and teamwork. The money raised will be used to expand activities which will help reduce the number of youths going astray. We must supply constructive outlets for the energies of our boys. Too many youngsters do not get the encouragement and understanding which is needed to spur them on.

The fund-raising campaign will run for a month. The community leaders who have been called for this dawn patrol breakfast must exert every effort within their communities and organizations to attain our goal. The goal can be attained if we reach our constituents with an intelligent appeal. With your help we will do our part to provide a world in which our boys can grow—unhindered and unwarped—into healthy, happy, normal human beings.

I believe it is one of our American privileges to support the fund appeal of the Boy Scouts. I am sure I can rely on your understanding and generosity to do the best you can in the current campaign for the Scouts and for our community and nation.

THANKING SPEAKER

I merely put into words what the audience's applause indicates. I should like to express to the Mayor our gratitude for coming to speak to us.

CLOSING

May I close with this observation:

The development of our youth is primarily a community problem. We must think of the problem from the long-range point of view. Solutions to be lasting must be built on firm foundations. The problem cannot be solved by some rapid or spectacular method. The Boy Scout movement is as sound an answer to our dilemma as anybody has been able to propose.

All contributions collected from your organizations and from individuals should be sent to the Scout office in the Walton Hotel, to assure our deserving lads success in the character-building program.

Thank you for coming.

26. The Big Brother Fund Drive

OPENING

We celebrate the fifth anniversary of the Big Brother Athletic Association's founding by honoring one of its benefactors and supporters. The Association was formed five years ago to provide a year-round program for boys and girls of the community between the ages of six and thirteen. The object has been to combat juvenile delinquency. During the five years of its existence two thousand boys and girls have enrolled, and they have enjoyed sports activities ranging from basketball to shuffleboard. They have also had the benefit of a year-round club, a summer camp, and health and vocational activities.

INTRODUCING SPEAKER

And now I present to you a director of the Big Brother movement who serves it in a very responsible position. He has an avid interest in young people and has been identified with youth agencies for more than twenty years. For years he has directed the energies of youth into proper channels. Mr. Thomas Tindall.

ADDRESS

The Big Brother Athletic Association is an undertaking worth knowing about and supporting. It is devoted to training boys and girls who might otherwise be left to their own resources in the ways of citizenship.

Public apathy, lack of recreation programs and of proper training, combine—even without slums or broken homes—to create unwholesome breeding places for juvenile delinquency.

The clubs formed by the Big Brother Athletic Association are an effective way to provide recreation. Citizens who offer their services to these Big Brother movements perform a worthwhile service.

The mainstay of these clubs is generally the secretary. What are the duties of a Big Brother secretary? It's one of those million-and-one detail jobs. He must see that the kids are properly outfitted with suits and equipment which are not left behind or taken away; that the children do not play on empty stomachs; that danger of injury on the athletic field is removed and that those injuries which can't be prevented are not serious. Then there are the duties involving personnel and finance. Too often he is called on to help raise funds. Fund-raising and athletics, separately and together, are not new to him.

Our guest of honor has devoted himself without stint to extending opportunities to boys and girls and to promote their growth and development into happier, self-sustaining members of the community.

INTRODUCING CIVIC LEADER

Our next speaker is chairman of numerous welfare and philanthropic committees for the benefit of youth organizations. He derives real satisfaction from working with young people and providing them with leadership and friendship during the formative years. He has devoted himself to helping people on a neighborhood level, making better citizens, creating better social conditions and offering those who might be lonely a feeling of belonging to the community. His is a hard but rewarding task. I am pleased to present Mr. Frank Smith.

MEDALLION PRESENTATION

It is my privilege to present to you on behalf of the Big Brother Athletic Association this medallion to commemorate your outstanding achievements. We also publicly express our admiration and gratitude for the great contribution you have made to the welfare of our community. This medallion is in recognition of our enduring gratitude. Let me describe it so that all here may know: It is three inches in diameter. It is of gold. The face bears a likeness of you, head and shoulders. On the reverse, the citation reads: "Presented to Joyce Jones by his many admiring friends in the Big Brother Athletic Association and in the community, for leadership in the youth movement and in recognition of his signal service to the community, especially to the Big Brother Athletic Association."

This community is the better for your magnificent public service, your devotion to duty, your intense interest in youth, your unflagging zeal in their behalf, your selflessness in serving others.

This medallion is a token of our esteem and appreciation for your great contribution to the welfare of our community. We wish for you many years to enjoy God's choicest blessings.

ACCEPTING MEDALLION

I am pleased and complimented by your words and the great honor implicit in the medallion presented to me. I appreciate it very much. This is a heart-warming demonstration. There are few things a man can do that would provide him with so many satisfactions. There are, first of all, the countless wonderful friendships acquired. There is the rewarding experience of working with men and women such as you. I entertain doubt as to whether I really deserve all this. However, that does not lessen my pleasure in these tributes and your very generous words of praise and commendation. I thank you all.

27. Induction of a Mayor

OPENING

We extend a warm welcome to all who by their presence here are honoring our newly elected Mayor. I will not infringe on your time and patience by any lengthy remarks. I am sure you are here because of a sense of responsibility to the community and the desire to extend good wishes to our guest of honor, Henry Alton.

INTRODUCING INSTALLING OFFICER

Judge Lawton will be the installing officer. It gives me pleasure to extend to him the gavel with which he will conduct the proceedings.

INSTALLING MAYOR

It is an honor and distinction to become Mayor of Centerville. The office of Mayor requires experience, ability, and fortitude. We are fortunate, indeed, that you, Henry Alton, have been selected again by the citizens of this community to this highest office. By dint of your energy and ability you have achieved a notable career. Your busy professional life did not preclude your active participation in community life, whether it be charitable, religious, civic or political. Small wonder then that so many people have gathered here to honor you. It is now my function, as installing officer, to induct you into office as Mayor to succeed yourself. I know that the leadership which you again assume is in very safe and capable hands. And now with my best wishes and with confidence in your continued success, I will administer the oath of office:

> "You do solemnly swear that you will perform the duties of the office of Mayor for the ensuing four years to the best of your ability."

INTRODUCING SPEAKER

I am quite sure that there are many people here who would like to give expression to the feeling they have toward Mayor Alton. I will now call upon Mr. Dan Daniels, President of the Centerville Civic Association.

TRIBUTE

I am here to bring the newly elected Mayor the greetings and good wishes of the citizens of Centerville. The Mayor has been an active participant in the affairs of Centerville for many years. His record as Mayor is one of which any man might be proud. He is one of our most useful citizens because he has the three vital I's—imagination, ingenuity, and industry. We all have a high regard for his courtesy, integrity, and fairness and for his laudable achievements. We wish him well.

INTRODUCING MAYOR

I do not have to say very much about the Mayor. He has the respect of the citizens because of his fine record. He has brought distinction to himself by the competent administration of the office of Mayor. His administration has received widespread recognition. He has the ability to be the mayor of any city. He is performing a great service to the community and we are fortunate that he has many years of useful service ahead of him. It is now my pleasure to call upon Mayor Alston.

ACCEPTANCE

I am grateful to the residents for re-electing me to the office of Mayor. I am grateful to my many supporters. My aim is to perform the functions of the office which I am about to re-assume so that the residents will fully enjoy living in this community. I promise that I will always try to do justice honestly, conscientiously and fairly.

I want to thank you, Judge Lawton, for presiding at these proceedings. I am indeed grateful to all of the members of the community gathered here today. It is a happy day in my life. But joy and happiness are never complete unless they are shared. In that respect I am indeed very fortunate. Assembled here today are many of my good friends, my lovely wife and children. I know if there is such a thing as vicarious happiness they certainly share it today. May I thank all of my good friends who have taken time off from their businesses and who have left their clients and patients to honor me by their presence. Thank you.

28. Induction of a Judge

It is a great pleasure to preside at this induction cere-mony and to share the joy of the family and friends of the new judge in the honor which has come to him. The Very Reverend John Houston will deliver the prayer.

INVOCATION

Almighty and Eternal God, who in Thyself art justice, truth and mercy, grant that Thy servant on whom Thou hast bestowed this special honor may have the knowledge of earthly law, a quick comprehension, and an under-standing and enlightened heart and mind which are necessary for him to carry out his office so that true justice may reign in every action he performs. We ask Thy special blessing on this occasion so that from henceforth he shall be one of Your own in true justice, truth and mercy. Amen.

INTRODUCING SPEAKER

Our speaker is president of the local Bar Association. He is here to salute the new judge and pay tribute to him. I present Mr. Bernard Brooks.

PRESENTING JUDICIAL ROBE

I join with you in honoring the man whose personal integrity and determination, whose wisdom and courage, and whose warm personal response to the problems of human individuals have brought him this recognition. I wish him many more steps up the judicial ladder.

The task of the judge is to administer justice fairly, competently, speedily, impartially and equally under the law.

Judge Law brings to this Court a wealth of experience. He brings to judicial service all the virtues we hope for in a judge—great knowledge and insight. He has an enviable capacity, as expressed by Matthew Arnold, to "see straight and think clear" which in the last analysis is one of the most valuable attributes possessed by a judge.

On behalf of the members of the Bar Association, I am pleased to present this judicial robe to you, Judge Law, as a symbol of the esteem and affection the officers and members of the Bar Association have for you. We know you will wear it well and gracefully. The Bar Association congratulates you and wishes you a very successful and a happy career.

INTRODUCING PRESENTER OF GIFT

The faculty, staff, students and friends of the Blackstone Law School glory in the elevation of a member of the faculty to judicial office. Mr. Sam Smith, Dean of the Law School, will make a presentation to the judge.

PRESENTING GAVEL

On behalf of the Blackstone Law School and in appreciation for your very valuable services to it, I present this gavel to you. It is inscribed: "Presented to Judge Harold Law by the faculty, members of the staff, and students of Blackstone Law School upon his induction as City Judge."

Gavels are appropriate as symbols. I know that decorum will be properly maintained in your courtroom without the necessity of using the gavel. We know that you will wield it in a manner that will bring credit to you.

As a member of our faculty, you are not only well-versed in law, but you have observed and followed the precepts laid down by the prophet Moses as recorded in Deuteronomy enjoining upon all judges, "Hear the causes between your brethren and judge righteously between every man and his brother and that stranger that is with him. Ye shall not respect persons in judgment but you shall hear the small as well as the great. Ye shall not be afraid of the face of man for the judgment is that of God."

I am sure that I express the sentiments of everyone in the Law School when I say that it is a great joy and pleasure to see you rewarded with this emblem of authority. May I add that you richly deserve this honor.

PRESENTING NEW JUDGE

Now, I come to my final act as presiding officer and the pleasant duty of presenting the new judge. He is a personal friend. I have the greatest respect and admiration for his ability. I have complete confidence that all our great expectations of him will be fulfilled. He is intolerant of any lapse of personal integrity. He is a believer in the simple virtues. And so it is with great pride that I present the man that all of us are here to honor, Judge Harold Law.

APPRECIATION AND THANKS

This is one of the happiest days of my life. But joy and happiness are never complete unless they are shared. In that respect I am indeed fortunate. Assembled here today are many of my good friends and members of my family. All of you were very kind to take time off to come here. Your kindness and the warmth of your friendship will not be forgotten.

I am deeply gratified and moved by the confidence expressed by the Mayor in appointing me to this position. My heartfelt thanks to the members of the clergy, the Mayor, and all the wonderful friends who gave me so much encouragement and advice down through the years. I especially thank my wife, Joan, who has always worked shoulder to shoulder with me. I assure you that I shall do everything in my power to justify the faith and confidence you have in me. I realize the grave duties and great responsibility that have been entrusted to me. I hope that I will justify the confidence of my friends. I will always try to do justice, honestly, conscientiously and fairly. In the language of my oath of office, I "will faithfully discharge my duties to the best of my ability."

I am reminded of the Biblical episode related in the First Book of Kings, in which the Lord appeared to Solomon and declared that He would grant him one request. Solomon responded: "O Lord, grant unto me an understanding heart that I might judge Thy people." I humbly join in that simple prayer.

I will treasure the robe and gavel that have been so generously given to me. These gifts, I regard as symbolic of the dignity and prestige of this court. I am sincerely and deeply grateful. May I thank you, Judge Rate, for the wonderful way you presided over the induction ceremony and my thanks to Mr. Bernard Brooks for his complimentary remarks and the presentation of the robe of office. Again, thank you for coming here.

READING CONGRATULATORY MESSAGES

We shall conclude these ceremonies with a benediction by Reverend Lane, but before its pronouncement I will read congratulatory messages received from Governor Stone and Senator Smith:

> "I was greatly pleased to learn of your appointment as Judge of the City Court. Please accept my warm congratulations and very best wishes at the outset of what I am confident will prove a long and successful career on the Bench.
>
> Steven Stone, Governor"

> "My very warmest congratulations to you upon your elevation to Judge of the City Court. The people of the county are fortunate to have a judge of your distinction and eminent qualifications. All the best to you.
>
> Senator Seymour Smith"

Thank you and good day to all.

BENEDICTION

Almighty God, Who didst create the universe with divine attributes of justice and mercy and Who art the ultimate judge of all who live and breathe, we ask Thy blessing upon Thy servant, Harold Law, who has just been solemnly inducted into his high office and who this day ascends the Bench to judge between his fellows by the will of his fellow citizens. May God grant him faith, wisdom and courage in all his acts. We who know him well and love him much are proud of him this day. We who are gathered here share warmly the pride and joy of those near and dear to him. And we pray unto Thee that he will continue, as he has until now, to find grace and good understanding in the eyes of God and of his fellow-men. Grant him and his family long life and health and happiness. Amen!

29. United Nations Anniversary Ceremony

OPENING

The United Nations is celebrating the anniversary of its founding. We live in what Toynbee, the great British historian, calls "a time of trouble." But there are compensations as inspiring as the birth of the United Nations.

The President of the United States of America, by proclamation, has urged the citizens of this nation to observe United Nations Day with community programs to demonstrate their faith and support of the United Nations and to create a better public understanding of its aims. As Mayor, I have implemented this with a similar proclamation urging the citizens of this community to observe United Nations Day in appropriate manner.

The United Nations represents man's most determined and promising effort to save humanity from the scourge of war and to promote conditions of peace and well-being for all nations. Our government believes that the United Nations deserves our continued firm support and that its success depends not only on the support given by its members, but equally on that of the peoples of the member countries.

The founding of the United Nations in 1945 was the beginning of world unity. We hope the U. N. will go on to use its vital influence toward the salvation of civilization.

The United Nations, man's best hope for a lasting peace, needs the active support of every community, every group, every organization, every individual. As good citizens, it is clearly our duty to foster an intelligent interest in our Government's policies within the United Nations and to develop an informed, dynamic public opinion in support of United States participation in the world organization.

It is proper to mark a milestone of such importance as an anniversary, but the United Nations is a year-round force working for peace and security 365 days a year. It needs your full-time backing and continuing support.

May I quote from the inspiring message of the late Dag

Hammarskjold, Secretary General of the United Nations:

"Mankind united in peaceful competition, free from fear and free from want, a mankind where man has truly come into his own—this great dream is exacting. It may demand great sacrifices. But it demands the deepest loyalty of every man. Short of our unreserved devotion, it will remain a dream, lacking substance. If this is not recognized, it may even blind us to reality and become a danger, though it should be a source of strength.

"May the trials and triumphs alike strengthen our resolve . . . to serve the cause of humanity with the unswerving loyalty and devotion that are demanded of us."

INTRODUCING PROGRAM CHAIRMAN

The U. N. Day Program Committee has devoted much time and energy to developing this program. The Chairman of the Committee, who will next speak to you, is tireless in her devotion to the U. N. She took an active role in stimulating popular support for the formation of the United Nations. She saw the United Nations grow, painfully, slowly. At each faltering step, she was there to lend a hand, to join with others to build a strong, enduring body. She has done much to help bring a better understanding of the aims and purposes of the United Nations. It is therefore with a great degree of pleasure that I present our Program Chairman who will deliver the address dedicating the United Nations Tree, Mrs. Vivian Vail.

DEDICATING UNITED NATIONS TREE

The civic, religious, patriotic and educational organizations of this community have taken an active part in stimulating popular support for the United Nations. These groups have employed their influence to impress the community with the vital importance of the U. N. They've helped bring about a better understanding of the aims and purposes of the U. N. It is the responsibility of every loyal American citizen to bring support to this instrument of world community.

The U. N. charter is not a perfect instrument for settling international disputes. But it does provide a forum for discussion of those disputes, and talking is always better than fighting. We would all do better if we emphasized its successes rather than its deficiencies. Many people do not feel that the United Nations is the solution, but it is by far the best, if not the only, organization that we have endeavoring to bring an end to world combat.

The aim of the United Nations is to organize the peace-loving nations of the world so that they will deter an aggressive nation from starting a war. We hope that can be done through the U. N.

Never in the world's history has so much power been amassed—not for the purposes of aggression and war, but solely for defense and peace. We have partnership arrangements for security with most of the world's nations. A fine record of accomplishment has been built. An optimistic outlook of much greater accomplishment in the future is no mere whistling in the dark. One thing is certain. The U. N. is the one solid hope of humanity for a peaceful and better world, and the United States can and must be its strongest supporter.

It is meet and proper that we dedicate the tree in the Town Hall Plaza as United Nations Tree and I symbolically so dedicate it. This marker will be set in front of the tree for all to see.

THANKING COMMITTEE

I cannot let this opportunity pass without expressing the appreciation of the civic, religious, and patriotic organizations of the community for the very active, intelligent, and hard work which has been done by the Chairman and other members of the Committee, not only this year, but in other years.

CLOSING

This program has been designed to provide you with means for informing yourself of vital issues so that you may be a more effective instrument for peace. We trust our aim has had some measure of success. We strongly believe in the power and responsibility of the individual for promoting peace.

30. Human Rights Day Observance

OPENING

Because you live in the U.S.A., you have certain rights protected by law. You can worship as you please, write and speak freely. No one can break into your home or drag you off to jail in secret. These are only a few of your American rights. Few people in the world have such rights. In many countries, rulers gag and terrorize the people, silencing all opposition to aggression and war. When this happens, peace is threatened. For that reason, the United Nations has adopted a Universal Declaration of Human Rights.

The work for human rights calls for a combination of high ideals and an awareness of existing realities. While celebrating the contribution of the Declaration on Human Rights, individuals should also accept our common responsibility for all that remains to be done over the years to bring the standards closer to universal practice. The Declaration which was adopted in Paris in 1948 is the culmination of centuries of struggle for human freedom. Adoption of the Declaration means recognition of these rights, not by force of arms on the battlefield, but by means of reason in a parliament of nations.

Our guest speaker has been active in preserving the right to print, teach, speak, assemble, petition and worship. He has never shown fear of any person or thing that interferes with free men in the exercise of their prerogatives. It pleases me to present to you, Mr. Jay Judson.

ADDRESS

The nations which signed the United Nations Charter at San Francisco specifically stated that the promotion and protection of human rights, formerly vested in nation states, should now also be an international responsibility.

The Charter's declaration of conscience won it a place on the revered scroll of events commemorating forward steps in this struggle—the Magna Carta in 1215, the Habeas Corpus Act of 1679, the Bill of Rights in 1776, the French Declaration of the Rights of Man in 1789.

The Atlantic Charter of 1941 expressed the hope that a peace might be established which would afford assurance that men in all lands might live out their lives in freedom from fear and want. The Washington Conference of 1942, the Moscow Conference of 1943, the Conversations at Dumbarton Oaks in 1944, gave assurances to the still struggling world that the conflict would end with the enthronement of human rights.

The Universal Declaration of Human Rights was adopted by the Third Committee of the General Assembly on December 7, 1948. The thirty articles of the Declaration set forth man's inalienable rights in the civil, political, economic, social and cultural fields; the right to life, liberty and security of person; to freedom from arbitrary arrest; to a fair trial; to privacy; to freedom of movement and residence; to social security; to work; to education; to a nationality; to freedom of worship; to freedom of expression and of peaceful assembly; to man's right to take part in the government of his own country; to hold public office; to seek and to be granted asylum; and to own property. The Assembly proclaimed these rights as "a common standard of achievement for all peoples and all nations."

It is hard to believe that there was a time (and not too long ago, historically speaking) when such rights could be withdrawn at the whim of an autocratic ruler. It is hard to realize that there are people today who do not have these rights. It is not easy for members of a free world to comprehend the difficulties of living under a police state, where a word that slips out in an unguarded moment can result in an ominous knock on the door in the dead of night.

Get to know the thirty rights which the United Nations has adopted as the Universal Declaration of Human Rights. It is not a code of law, but a statement of principles. These thirty rights may reshape the world.

THANKING THE SPEAKER

I know of no better way to express appreciation of a great exposition of a vital subject than doing what you did by your generous applause. We are indebted to Mr. Judson for his interesting talk.

CLOSING

Nothing that concerns the well-being of our fellow-men can be of indifference to us. There is always one race, the human one. We are so much alike. The world we want is a world without prejudices, without selfishness; a world of understanding. We cannot have true peace until we have created a world without fear. The subject of the program is one of vital importance which is becoming more and more impressed upon every thoughtful citizen of this land.

31. Politics and You, the Citizen

OPENING

It is the purpose of this meeting to bring to you the facts concerning the issues of the local campaign and the qualifications of the candidates; and to call attention to the citizens' responsibilities.

INTRODUCING SPEAKER

Our speaker is a brilliant lawyer who was an effective assemblyman, a distinguished judge and is now the Attorney General. Our Attorney General is interested in the average citizen. He prosecutes slum lords, shady TV repairmen, fraudulent home-improvement contractors, and gyp charity drive promoters. He protects the wage earner, the home owner, the tenant, the civil service employee, and the legitimate businessman against fraudulent competition. He is one of the most vigorous and efficient Attorneys General in the history of our State. Honorable John Jones will address you.

ADDRESS

Election Day is the day when each of us can participate in our government—the day when we are called upon to help make the final decision. When one neglects to vote, he hands over his rights to others. He weakens the political system. Whatever one's politics may be, it is his duty to vote. We show our pride in our country by exercising our duties as citizens. Those who fail to exercise the right to vote don't show appreciation for the real greatness of America.

The importance of registration and enrollment cannot be too strongly stressed. In order to vote for the public officials who will govern you and enact laws by which you must abide—you must be registered. Many of us fail to register, not because of principle, but from laziness, forgetfulness, or simple annoyance. Many voters who register fail to enroll in the party of their choice. Many are suspicious of letting others know their party preference.

Others disdain to enroll because of a misguided notion that they are too good for it—that they are "independents." Independence in voting is a fine thing. But this country's government is built on a two-party system and no one can participate fully in the electoral process without being an enrolled party member. We believe in our two-party system because competition in politics makes for better politics, just as competition in business makes for better business. Without good candidates there is no real choice on Election Day. Enrollment does not, of course, curtail "independence." How one votes is a personal matter completely unaffected by whether one happens to belong to one party or the other. You do not surrender your independence when you join a political party. Not to enroll, is simply to deprive oneself of some of the privileges of citizenship.

There should be an end to that shopworn excuse that is offered for not registering: "After all, my one little vote wouldn't really count." Single ballots were crucial in California in 1916 when Woodrow Wilson carried the state over Charles Evans Hughes by less than 4,000 votes. Those 4,000 votes determined who would be President of the United States during one of the most critical periods in the history of mankind—that of World War I.

Communities are not likely to enjoy good government unless their citizens demand it—and registering, enrolling, and voting are indications of their interest.

CLOSING

It is your duty as citizens to register and vote. New voters especially should take an interest in the political and civic activities of their community. Only in that way can a firm foundation of informed, public-spirited citizens be established to accomplish community improvements. Close ties with political activities also will build better citizens of the future. There is a great need for young leadership in politics.

The lack of interest in politics on the part of women is a source of disappointment. I don't know the reason for that lack of interest, but it is there. If only women could appreciate the opportunity that is afforded to them in our political system! Women should be encouraged regardless of political ideology to participate in their community on a political level so that under our two-party system Democrats and Republicans will have the benefit of their participation.

Let us elevate the quality of our political leadership by showing more than a passive interest in our local government. Let our young men and women get into the midst of political life. The type of political leadership we get is merely a reflection of community standards.

You have probably been told many times that in a democracy like ours the people get the kind of government they ask for. If they pay little attention to political affairs, stay away from the polls on Election Day, try to avoid other obligations of citizenship, and in general devote all their time and energy to their own businesses, they are asking for corrupt and inefficient government—and they usually get it. On the other hand, if they are actively interested in public affairs, determined to have honest and capable men in office, and are willing to work hard to elect them, they will usually enjoy honest and reasonably efficient government.

32. Convention Proceedings

Please come to order. It is a distinct privilege to greet the members of the Communities Association who are here to participate in our discussions and deliberations. We have convened to hold the twenty-fifth annual meeting of the Association. I am confident that our convention will be successful and interesting and that our discussions will be pleasant, profitable, and a credit to the Association and will result in benefit to our communities. For myself, I hope to have your indulgence during the proceedings.

INTRODUCING CLERGYMAN

I am privileged to ask Reverend Rauch to deliver the invocation.

INVOCATION

Almighty God, our Heavenly Father, we beseech Thee to be here in this council assembled in Thy name and presence. We desire to commence and to continue and to conclude our discussions and deliberations in the remembrance of Thine own existence. We beseech Thee, also, to inspire all the members of the Communities Association with right and true ideals of the commendable work in which they are engaged. Direct the Association in all its deliberations and make them to succeed in all their efforts for the good of their community and the welfare of their fellow-citizens. We beseech Thee to direct us in all our doings with Thy gracious favor, that we may glorify Thy Holy name, and, finally, through Thy mercy, may obtain everlasting life. Amen!

INTRODUCING SPEAKER

The people of this city rightfully can be proud of what they have accomplished under the leadership of their Mayor. He has contributed effort and imagination to making this city the great gathering place it is. The growth and development of this metropolis is largely due to his ability. I present to you, for an address of welcome —Mayor Charles Carr.

WELCOME

I was honored by being asked to make the address of welcome. After I had accepted it, I was in a quandary as to what I could say after telling you how happy we are to have you come to our city. I looked through the bound volumes of the proceedings of your Association to see the addresses of welcome given by the various greeters at the annual meetings. I was somewhat surprised, for I found that the speakers in their addresses of welcome took up all their time in extolling the virtues of their particular section of the country. Their speeches read more like the real estate section of the Sunday newspaper than anything else. But I am not going to follow that custom. We are honored that your Association decided to hold its meetings here. For it is an honor. We have never anticipated any convention with more sincere pleasure than that of your Association. We hope you will enjoy what we have to the fullest extent. We hope you may grow in wisdom because of your meetings here and that you may accomplish those things that are dear to your hearts. Above all, we hope that your stay here will be so pleasant that when you return to your work and are grinding away, you will occasionally think of this city and your thoughts will cause you someday to return to us.

MINUTES

The minutes of the last Annual Meeting have been printed in the year book of which every member has a copy. Therefore, unless there is an objection, or someone wishes to have a correction noted, the minutes of that meeting stand approved.

INTRODUCING PAST PRESIDENT

It is traditional at this stage of the convention proceedings to hand the gavel of authority to the immediate past president who will act as chairman. I present with pleasure our immediate Past President, Mr. Ralph Ramon. (*Assumes chair.*)

INTRODUCING PRESIDENT

In accordance with the established order of business,

the President will now present his annual report. Mr. Harry Haven.

PRESIDENT'S ANNUAL REPORT

As we begin this twenty-fifth annual convention, may I express to you my heartfelt appreciation for your fine support during the past year. The opportunity to work with you has been a rare privilege—one that will linger long and pleasantly in my memory.

If you will review our record of accomplishments for the year, I think ample basis will be found for the belief that this Association is becoming more and more effective in its work and achievements. Although it is far from the goal which it sought to reach, I do think that year after year it is making steady progress toward that end. Your enthusiastic and active support of those ideals upon which this Association was founded is evidenced by the fact that an ever-increasing public are looking to us for help in their problems.

When you hear the reports of the various activities undertaken during the past year by your Association—and, when you take part in the discussions which will follow—you will readily understand why the Association is recognized as a leading force in improving our communities and correcting local evils and abuses. This is further evidenced by the large membership which represents a substantial increase since the convention which was held a year ago.

As I approach the end of my year as president, permit me to thank you most sincerely for the pleasure and profit which has come to me from that relationship, for your uniform kindness and courtesy, and your patience and forbearance with me.

TEMPORARY CHAIRMAN'S REMARKS

Those who have read the printed report of the work of this Association, of which the oral report you have just heard is a synopsis, must be convinced that the activities of the Association are many, its accomplishments large, and its responsibilities great.

I now call upon the Chairman of the Publicity Committee for his report.

PUBLICITY COMMITTEE REPORT

Ralph Waldo Emerson said, "If a man built a good mousetrap, even though he lived in a forest the world would make a path to his door." That was many years ago. The world has changed since then. It is essential now for a successful organization to keep in touch with the most powerful influence perhaps of modern times— the press and, of course, radio and television. That has been the scope of activities of our committee during the past year. It is not sufficient to keep in touch with the press during the meeting only, but throughout the entire year. Your committee during the past year has from time to time given to the press matters of interest and bulletins of varied character. We will gather together for this meeting all the important reports and speeches and put them in the hands of the press for release.

Your committee considers it of great importance to

bring before the country the activities of the Association and to impress upon it the high ideals for which the organization stands.

At this date, your committee is actively engaged in doing its share to make this annual meeting the greatest in the history of the organization.

ELECTION OF PRESIDENT

The next order of business is the election of the president. I will ask our Past President, Mr. Ralph Ramon, again to take the chair to conduct the election of president. (*Past president assumes chair.*)

CALL FOR NOMINATIONS

Nominations are now in order for president for the ensuing year. The Chair recognizes Mr. Martin Moss.

NOMINATION

I wish to place in nomination a man who has been tested. Every institution is judged by its elected representatives. This organization has been most fortunate in its officers. They have been loyal men of the very best judgment and character. I wish to emphasize the qualities of the man I have nominated. He is able, courageous, and loyal. It is my privilege to place before you for office of president, Mr. Harry Haven.

SECOND NOMINATION

(*Member from Convention floor.*) It is my privilege to second the nomination of Harry Haven, a great statesman, a champion of the dignity of man, who has conducted the affairs of this Association with great skill, ingenuity, and competence. He has captured the imagination of our membership and has endeared himself to all members who have had contact with him.

CLOSING NOMINATIONS AND BALLOTING

(*Member from floor*) I move that nominations be closed.

(*Member*)   I second the motion.

(*Chairman*)   All in favor, say "Aye." Those opposed, say "Nay." (*No response.*) The motion is approved.

(*Member*)   I move that the secretary be instructed to cast the ballot of this convention for the unanimous election of Harry Haven as president of this Association for the ensuing year.

(*Chairman*) The Secretary is instructed to cast the vote of the convention for the unanimous election of Harry Haven as president of Communities Association for the ensuing year. (*Secretary casts ballot.*) The Secretary having cast such ballot, I declare Harry Haven unanimously elected president of this Association for the ensuing year.

PRESENTING NEWLY RE-ELECTED PRESIDENT

I have the profound honor and the great personal pleasure to present to you your newly re-elected President. It is my privilege to yield to him the gavel symbolizing his authority. (*Hands over gavel.*)

ACCEPTANCE OF OFFICE

Of course, I am more deeply grateful than I can tell at receiving the honor of conducting in the coming year the activities of this great Association.

When I realize how our services and activities have increased in the past few years, and when I contemplate that you have selected me this year, I become frightened, and too, I become exceedingly humble.

The founders of this Association laid a great foundation. My eminent predecessors continued to build on that foundation, until the edifice which has arisen before us is exceedingly full of promise. If I can raise that edifice by even one story, I shall have succeeded. If I do not, I shall have failed.

In order to carry out our objectives, we will face many difficult and complicated problems. But I have confidence in this organization. I haven't the slightest doubt that we will continue to advance. As for myself, I will strive to give the presidency the best that I have. In the coming year, with your generous cooperation, I shall try to express some of the appreciation which I feel by endeavoring to carry on and further the splendid work of the Association. In that effort, I invite your criticism. I solicit your assistance. I thank you.

ANNOUNCEMENT BY PRESIDENT OF NOMINATION OF OFFICERS

The Committee on Nominations has recommended that

the following persons be elected to the offices which follow their names:

Frank Silk—Vice-President
Richard Scribe—Secretary
Fred Fund—Treasurer

I will entertain an appropriate motion. (*Follow procedure outlined above for election of President.*)

RESOLUTION OF APPRECIATION FOR HOSPITALITY

A resolution has been submitted which I will read and then submit for your decision:

"*Whereas*, the Mayor and other public officials, have warmly welcomed the officers, delegates and visitors of Communities Association to this Convention, and have truly outdone themselves in their efforts as cordial, generous and warm-hearted hosts; and

Whereas, the officers, delegates and guests of this Association are deeply thankful for the warm welcome and hospitality extended to them, therefore be it

Resolved, that the officers and delegates of this Convention of Communities Association extend their deep appreciation and sincere thanks to all those who have contributed toward making this an eminently successful and enjoyable Convention."

SUBMISSION OF MOTION

You have heard the resolution expressing our appreciation to the people of this community for the warm welcome and hospitality they have accorded our delegates during our stay here. If there is no objection, the resolution of thanks will be adopted. Hearing none, it is so ordered.

CLOSING

We have reached the hour of adjournment.

The committees which have served us so well are respectfully discharged with the thanks of this convention.

The meeting will be declared closed after the prayer, but before so doing I wish to thank most heartily all the members of the Association for the uniform courtesy and consideration shown me. I express my sincere appreciation to the delegates at this Convention for the very fine attendance we have had, and the rapt attention which they gave to the speakers. I wish you all a happy and safe journey home. Reverend Richard Rauch will pronounce the benediction.

BENEDICTION

Almighty Father, we beseech Thy blessings upon us. As we are about to adjourn our annual meeting and as we go our separate roads, guide us in Thy ways of truth and righteousness. Endow us with wisdom and strength to carry out our daily tasks. Bless all the members of our Association and their families; bless all the leaders of our country so that their decisions may prove beneficial to all mankind. God be with us till we meet again. Amen.

Section II

EXAMPLES OF
LABOR UNION CEREMONIES

33. Induction of Members

This should be a proud day for you. Your application for membership in Local 234, after due investigation, has been approved.

I take pleasure in presenting to you an officer of the Union who will induct you into membership. He has an understanding of labor problems and the respect and admiration of the community. He will, no doubt, tell you about this Union's history and the rights and privileges incidental to membership. Brother Richard Right.

We welcome you to membership in Local 234. Local 234 has a wonderful history. Many years ago a handful of members joined together for the purpose of improving conditions in the industry. Great sacrifices were made by them to realize their aims. The rise of the Union has often been compared with the rise of our Nation. Every American is acquainted with the story of how thirteen weak colonies won their freedom from the English kings by organizing themselves into a union of states. And as it was then, so it is true with us. These members, who were weak individually, united to get rid of unbearable conditions, and laid the foundation of our Union. But just as the thirteen states—once they won their freedom— grew to fifty powerful states composing the greatest Nation on earth, so our little Union has grown in membership, prestige and respect. Our members now have satisfactory economic conditions, vacations with pay, welfare and pension funds, insurance, sick and health benefits.

Before you can become a member, it will be necessary for you to take this pledge:

"I do hereby solemnly and sincerely pledge to perform the duties appertaining to my membership as prescribed by the laws of the International Union and of Local 234."

You are now members of the Union and I extend my heartiest congratulations.

CLOSING

This concludes the induction ceremonies. I offer my own congratulations. I have every confidence that you will conduct yourselves in a manner that will bring credit to you and your Union. You will be presented with a copy of our Union constitution. Read it, know it; let it be your guide.

34. Installation of Officers

We are here to install our newly-elected officers. The officers you elected have wide powers. They have been given the right to decide questions which will affect you, your families, your mode of living, your peace and happiness.

Our Union has a wonderful history. A great opportunity lies ahead to continue the high standard of its methods and objectives. You are part of an industry that has been a pillar of the American way of life—by upholding that way of life we can have a future as glorious as is our past.

The decisions of the officers you have elected must be wise and just. Fortunately, the officers you chose have the wisdom and knowledge for a successful and just administration.

INSTALLING PRESIDENT

The office of president requires a man of knowledge, ability and fortitude, and above all, a passion for justice. You have all these qualifications. The members are fortunate, indeed, that you have been selected to this important position. You have been chosen to lead them, to inspire them, and to guide them.

It is my function, as it is my privilege and pleasure, to install you into office. As I hand you the gavel, which is the emblem of your office, it is a great satisfaction to me to welcome you as the new president. You are alert, friendly, poised and confident. You are, in every way, worthy of the honor conferred upon you tonight. I know that the leadership which you now assume is in safe and capable hands. The gavel is now yours (*Hands over gavel.*) With it goes a warm welcome to our new leader and a pledge by every member to work with you toward the high goals of a new year. And now, with my best wishes and with every confidence in your success, I turn over to you the presidency and the captaincy of the organization. I will now administer the oath of office.

"I do hereby solemnly and sincerely pledge my honor, in the presence of the witnesses here assembled, to perform the duties appertaining to my office, as prescribed by the laws of the National Union to the best of my ability, and to bear true allegiance to the National. I do further pledge to deliver to my successor in office all books, papers and other property of the National Union that may be in my possession or under my control at the close of my official term. Further, I do solemnly swear [*or* affirm] that I am not a member of the Communist Party or any organization which advocates the overthrow of

the government of the United States or Canada
by force, violence or other subversive or uncon-
stitutional methods, and during my term of office
I will not knowingly aid or support the activities
of any such party or organization."

INSTALLING VICE-PRESIDENT

Our constitution provides that the Vice-President is to
perform all the duties of the President in his absence and
to take the chair whenever he requests. You have heard
me describe the powers and responsibilities of the office
of President. Those powers and responsibilities are also
yours. (*Administers oath.*)

INSTALLING SECRETARY

The skillful performance of your duties is of the greatest
importance to the welfare of the Union and its members.
The qualities which distinguish a good secretary are intelligence, prompt attention to business, integrity in all
his dealings with the Union and its members. The records
you prepare will be the monument by which your work
will be remembered. The office of secretary should be
given only to men of the strictest integrity. But once a
union has a true and trusted secretary, it should not dis-
pense with his services but continue to elect him as long
as he can be prevailed upon to serve. A union which has
secured for this office a man who is as interested in his
work, as you are, will do well to value him highly. (*Administers oath.*)

INSTALLING TREASURER

The treasurer's duties are to receive and be responsible for the safekeeping of and to account for the general funds of the Union. We know you will prudently preserve the funds of the organization. (*Administers oath.*)

INSTALLING EXECUTIVE BOARD

Each of you has been elected by the membership to serve two years on the all-important Executive Board. The responsibility of the Board cannot be overstated. It is often the court of last resort. Every member of the Board should make a determined effort to be just and fair. (*Administers oath.*)

CLOSING

In accepting leadership you, our new officers, have dedicated yourselves to the service of our Union. In return, the members pledge to work untiringly at your side in advancing the goals of trade unionism. We know that the great achievements of the past will be the basis for further advances in the future. Under the inspiring leadership of our new officers I am confident we will continue to prosper.

35. Retirement of Secretary

GREETING AND WELCOME

We have convened to pay tribute to Arthur Ogden upon his retirement as secretary after twenty-five years of service to our Union. He has well earned retirement. Much of the executive work, supervision, and direction in the past rested upon his shoulders.

It is fortunate for a union, or any organization, to have its welfare entrusted to a person as intelligent, enthusiastic, and efficient as Arthur. It is fitting that his retirement is not permitted to pass without paying our tributes of respect, appreciation, and affection. And it is infinitely more important that these tributes be paid while he can yet hear and enjoy them.

INTRODUCING SPEAKER

The person chosen to represent us in paying homage to Arthur Ogden is one of his colleagues. He occupies a distinguished position in the field of social service. Throughout his career he has rendered service to the labor movement and the community far beyond the call of duty. It is my pleasure to present Bernard Blake.

153

TRIBUTE

During installations we are accustomed to hear that the secretary assumes the duties of recording the proceedings. This seems a simple enough task, but in practice it really isn't. The discharge of the secretary's duties requires the talent and skill of a diplomat. It would be impossible to detail all his duties. He is charged with the responsibility of seeing that everything is maintained on an even keel.

Arthur, you are retiring from office but you cannot withdraw from the place which you hold in our hearts. The committee has a little gift for you. It is a diplomat's bag or attaché case. It is our hope that the Almighty God will fill it to overflowing with all the goodness and happiness in life. Good luck to you in retirement—to you and your family, all the happiness in the world. We certainly are going to miss you.

INTRODUCING GUEST OF HONOR

The retirement of an official who has so loyally and efficiently served his organization for as long a time as has Arthur Ogden is a great loss. We are distressed to see him go, but the best wishes of the Board and every member go with him in retirement. We are all hopeful that he will have many fine, happy years. I now call upon our guest of honor, Arthur Ogden.

FAREWELL ADDRESS

The twenty-five years I have served as your secretary have been full of richly rewarding experiences. I am grateful to have had the opportunity to serve, and I have deep regrets at giving it up—no matter how compelling are my reasons for so doing. I consider the position I held as one of great honor. I hope that my efforts have met with some measure of success.

I thank you for the cooperation which you have given me during my term of office. Especially, I want you to know that I appreciate the good-will and services of the members of our Executive Board. There has never been an Executive Board so able, cooperative, and sympathetic.

From the bottom of my heart I thank you for all that you have so generously said about my accomplishments, for the courtesy you have shown me by coming here, and for the splendid gift which I will always treasure. To-night's demonstration of your affection is in itself compensation for my twenty-five years of service. I am honored and touched. It is good to have lived and worked with you all. Thank you very much.

CLOSING

Because of the conflicting schedules, many who would have liked to be here could not come, but sent messages which I will read. After the reading of the messages this event will be concluded. (*Messages are read.*)

36. Testimonial to Officer

The presence this evening of so many is convincing proof of the high regard in which all of us hold Benjamin Lane. His career has been one of service to his fellow-man.

INTRODUCING SPEAKER

I present to you the President of Local 234 who is largely responsible for his Union's present position of influence. He has the respect and admiration not only of the members of his own Union, but of all trade unionists with whom he works. He is a civic-minded individual and a humanitarian. I present Brother Foster Brown.

TRIBUTE

It is fitting on this occasion that we take note of Benjamin Lane's excellent service to our Union for more than twenty-five years. It is largely to him that we owe the existence of our organization. He was one of the founders. In his fertile brain was born the idea of establishing an organization of workingmen. To carry out that purpose, he gathered around him a group of capable and idealistic workers whose labors culminated in the formation of the Union. His interest in it has never waned. We greatly appreciate all that he accomplished and his genius in guiding the Union to its present position of influence.

His many civic activities include directorships in Hope Hospital, Home for the Aged, and Camp for the Underprivileged. He is a man with a remarkable ability to inspire personal loyalty and affection. He well deserves the tributes accorded him.

It is a privilege for me to present to him this medal for "Long and honorable service to the members of Local 234, and the people of the community."

RESPONDING TO TRIBUTE

The years I served as an officer of Local 234 have proved among my most stimulating experiences. I am happy that I have the good opinion and esteem of the members, my associates and my friends.

I will always recall the events of this evening with a glow of pride and satisfaction. I feel that whatever I accomplished was due in no small measure to the friendships I made. All my friends guided and helped. I am exceedingly grateful for the compliments and the medal. It is at such a moment that I humbly give thanks to the Almighty for the blessings that have been granted me. God bless you, and keep every one.

CLOSING

Our Union will continue to move along, increasing in

prestige and influence and dedicated to the promotion of a happier, healthier, and more peaceful world for all. We are thankful that we have been blessed with the devoted leadership of the man we honor tonight. Everyone in the industry, worker and employer, wishes Benjamin Lane success and satisfaction in all his undertakings. I hope you have enjoyed the salute to a man we admire. Good night.

37. Unveiling a Plaque

OPENING

We are here to show in an enduring way our appreciation of the life and achievements of the late Frank Farr, a labor statesman and a man of integrity, for the many years of service to the community and his Union. He firmly believed that community service is a vital part of trade unionism. Unions, indeed, are more than instrumentalities for collective bargaining purposes. They are voluntary associations of free men and women designed to meet human needs—outside as well as within the place of employment.

Frank Farr's untimely passing last year was a tragedy to both trade unionism and the community.

INTRODUCING SPEAKER

I have the pleasant duty to present to you, as our speaker, an outstanding citizen of the community who has had a long and distinguished career in the labor movement. He has a deep and profound interest in the betterment of all peoples. He is president of the Craft Union and is giving it excellent leadership. He is charting its course with great skill, ingenuity and statesmanship. He will make the presentation of a plaque on behalf of Local 10 of which Frank Farr had been president. I present Brother John Jones.

PRESENTING PLAQUE

It is a privilege to be chosen to present this plaque on behalf of Local 10. It describes the laudable achievements of the late Frank Farr. It is proper to place this memorial at the portal of this hall where it will be seen and read by all who enter here. It expresses in some small way the gratitude of the community and the esteem and affection in which he is held by both labor and management. If this plaque serves to keep alive an appreciation of the greatness of Frank Farr and his accomplishments it will, indeed, have been fruitful. It will have well repaid the wisdom and initiative of those who have placed it here. I will read the inscription.

> "For his long and honorable devotion to the welfare and good of his community. His creative vision, executive ability and patriotic interest in America brought him many honors. He

showed that labor is always ready to help organize the total community for health, welfare and recreation services. Among the fields which benefited from his efforts are: education, replacement of slums by better housing, medical research and mental health. His conspicuous service to his Union merits the recognition of its officers and members and this expression of appreciation."

INTRODUCING PROGRAM CHAIRMAN

Our enterprising and efficient Program Chairman will make the formal acceptance. Brother Frank Fulton.

ACCEPTANCE

The late Frank Farr had a place in the hearts of the members of his Union and the citizens of the community. His life will ever be an inspiration to us. By his efforts the range of Union services was broadened and intensified. For many years he was in the vanguard of the struggle against bigotry, intolerance, prejudice and injustice. He had a determination to help abolish inequities and redress wrongs. He had a tenacious loyalty to the principles of liberalism. He was a tireless seeker and lover of peace. He will long be remembered by the community and the labor movement. Those whom he helped and those who will continue to be helped through his planning and efforts will be his lasting monument. On behalf of the Labor Temple, I gratefully accept this plaque as a memorial to our beloved Frank Farr.

CLOSING

It is proper that we give public recognition of the lifetime of service rendered by the late Frank Farr and his contributions to American life. He gave of himself, unselfishly, in the fight for first-class citizenship for all, for help to our aged, for housing for the homeless, for food for the hungry, and for recognition of basic values.

38. Unveiling a Portrait

GREETING AND WELCOME

I extend a very hearty welcome to all. We are here to attend the formal presentation of a portrait of Maxwell Jones painted by the distinguished artist Raymond Ramon. These ceremonies are being sponsored by Craft Union of which Maxwell Jones is a past president.

I have known Maxwell Jones for more than twenty years. His life has been so rich and so full that no limited time could contain even a bare catalogue of his achievements. I shall simply mention his deep interest in labor, in worthy causes, in government; his great sense of humor, enthusiasm, unflagging zeal, intelligence, and his integrity. He has set an example of public service to his community.

INTRODUCING PROGRAM CHAIRMAN

We owe a debt of gratitude to our program chairman for his boundless enthusiasm and invaluable assistance in many ways. He has been asked to make the presentation of the portrait of our guest of honor. It is a privilege to present—Mr. Richard Morrow.

UNVEILING PORTRAIT

When a man stands heads and shoulders above the crowd there are good reasons for it. As president of the Craft Union, Maxwell Jones brought to that position his long experience. To the solution of problems of the Union, he brought a keen and logical mind. His energy and drive gave new impetus to the Union's leadership. His vision and sound judgment have helped to steer the ship of the organization on a true course away from dangerous shoals. In his social and communal activities, he has established a rare pattern—a combination of humility and dignity, courtesy and firmness, kindness and devotion to duty.

Maxwell Jones possesses rare qualities of character. He has been a source of inspiration to many of us. To me, personally, he has been a man's most valued treasure —a loyal friend. I know of no one in the community who is more respected and admired than is Max.

In unveiling the portrait of a true gentleman whose career has been so full of inspiration and whose future still lies ahead of him, we perform an act that is and will become even more significant in time to come. Mr. Jones, we are proud to honor you who have brought so much honor to us. We wish you and your family good health and happiness and many, many years in which to enjoy the respect and admiration of your fellow-citizens. Now, before I remove the veil from the portrait, I would like to read the legend on the brass plate attached to the frame:

"Maxwell Jones, president of Craft Union: presented by his friends in acknowledgement and appreciation of the true, faithful, and outstanding services rendered by him."

I take pleasure in unveiling the portrait and presenting it to the Labor Temple. This is a rare and unusual happening, since it marks a gracious expression of appreciation which is usually indulged in only after the completion of a man's activities. This portrait is a symbol of our affection and love for Maxwell Jones.

It was for these reasons that we decided it would be proper that a portrait of Maxwell Jones be painted to take its place with those of his predecessors in office. The artist has done his work nobly. A good portrait is said to be a kind of biography. You are about to see it and can judge for yourselves.

In the years to come, I hope this portrait will serve as an ever-continuing inspiration and that there will be many others who will deserve perpetuation of their features on these walls. I am sure it is a satisfaction to all of his friends that the portrait of Maxwell Jones is displayed in a prominent place in the Hall of the Labor Temple.

THANKING PROGRAM CHAIRMAN

If all of the members of the Union knew, as some of us do, of the very arduous labors performed by Mr. Richard Morrow during the past year, you would share with us real gratitude for his very successful efforts. The thanks of the Union go to him for the conscientious and fruitful work he has done.

INTRODUCING GUEST OF HONOR

It is the duty of the toastmaster to introduce the speakers in brief terms. Although I could say a good deal more about our guest of honor, I will limit myself to presenting him to you as one who contributed to making our community a citadel of promise—our guest of honor, Maxwell Jones.

ACCEPTANCE AND THANKS

I am overwhelmed that I have been thought worthy of so great an honor. I am deeply touched because this is the first time I have been so honored.

The artist who painted this portrait is to be congratulated on what he has done. He did a marvelous job with a very poor subject. This portrait hangs among my distinguished predecessors. If you are to remember me at all, I hope that the recollection will be of one who tried to do the best he could. I assure you that it will always be a matter of great pride to have my portrait in the Hall of the Labor Temple.

I deeply appreciate Brother Morrow's kindness in making the presentation. I am indebted to you, Mr. Chairman, for the excellent way in which you officiated at these impressive ceremonies. Thank you all.

CLOSING

It has been an honor for me to preside at this event. It has been a privilege to work in daily contact with the guest of honor. No president of the Union has faced more of the organization's problems or was better equipped to deal with them. We fervently hope that it is the will of Providence that he enjoy many fruitful years.

39. Politics and the Member

OPENING

It is the purpose of this meeting to encourage union members to take an active interest in politics. Election Day is the day when each of us can participate in our government—the day when we are called upon to help make the final decision. When one neglects to vote he hands over the rights of running the government. He weakens the political system which is important to his way of life in a free country. Whatever one's politics may be, and whether or not he thinks his choice among the candidates has a chance of election, it is his duty to vote.

We show our pride in our country by exercising our duties as citizens. The very foundation of our country is built on the right to vote, and those who don't exercise that right, don't appreciate the real greatness of America.

INTRODUCING LABOR LEADER

Our speaker holds a distinguished place in the labor world. Through the years of trials and tribulations that have beset the men and women of American labor, he has made a contribution that will not be forgotten. It is my distinct pleasure to present Mr. Murray Charles.

ADDRESS ON PRACTICAL POLITICS

When I am introduced in a way such as your chairman has introduced me, I feel that I may have difficulty in realizing your expectations.

The coming election is of utmost importance to every member. The importance of registration and enrollment cannot be too strongly stressed. In order to vote for the public officials who will govern you and enact laws by which you must abide—you must be registered. Many of us fail to register because of laziness, forgetfulness, or simple annoyance. Many voters who register fail to enroll in the party of their choice. Many are suspicious of letting others know their party preference. Others disdain to enroll because of a misguided notion that they are too good for it—that they are "independents." Independence in voting is a fine thing. But this country's government is built on a two-party system and no one can participate fully in the electoral process without being an enrolled party member. We believe in our two-party system because competition in politics makes for better politics just as competition in business makes for better business. Without good candidates, there is no real choice on Election Day. Enrollment does not, of course, curtail "independence." How one votes is a personal matter, completely unaffected by whether one happens to belong to one party or the other. You do not surrender your independence when you join a political party. Not to enroll, is simply to deprive one's self of some of the privileges of citizenship.

Communities are not likely to enjoy good government unless its citizens demand it—and registering, enrolling, and voting are indications of their interest.

THANKING SPEAKER

In common with you, I have listened with the greatest interest to the speaker, Mr. Murray Charles, whose address is thoughtful, informative, and able. I trust his plea will be heeded. We want everybody who is eligible to register and vote in the elections because we want the decision of America, not the decision of the minority.

CLOSING

It is your duty as a citizen to register and vote. New voters especially should take an interest in the political and civic activities of their country. Only in that way can a firm foundation of informed, public-spirited citizens be established to accomplish community improvements. Close ties with political activities also will build better citizens of the future. There is a great need for young leadership in politics

Let us elevate the quality of our political leadership by showing more than a passive interest in our local government. Let our young men and women get into the midst of political life. The type of political leadership we get is merely a reflection of community standards.

You have probably been told many times that in a democracy like ours the people get the kind of government they ask for. If they pay little attention to political affairs, stay away from the polls on Election Day, try to avoid other obligations of citizenship, and in general devote all their time and energy to their own businesses, they are asking for corrupt and inefficient government—and they usually get it. On the other hand, if they are actively interested in public affairs, determined to have honest and capable men in office, and are willing to work hard to elect them, they will usually enjoy honest and reasonably efficient government.

40. Labor Day Observance

OPENING

The local unions have been asked by the national organizations to lead suitable observances of Labor Day to remind all Americans of their priceless right as citizens. Labor Day is a national holiday dedicated to the wage earners of America. In recent years it has not been given the prominence it deserves as a national holiday by members of organized labor because of the many other attractions that are presented on this day.

The man credited with the idea of setting aside a holiday for this purpose is Peter J. McGuire, the founder of the Carpenters Union, who called for a day to "be established as a general holiday for the laboring classes." His idea bore fruit. The first Labor Day started with a giant parade and ended with a picnic festival to show publicly "the strength and *esprit de corps* of the trade and labor organizations."

Unfortunately, Labor Day has lost the original quality that made it exclusively The Day of the American worker. It has become a great national holiday marking the end of summer vacation and the beginning of the serious work of the fall and winter. It is a day that now ranks with the greatest of American holidays. But it is a day that should have special meaning to the organized worker.

INTRODUCING SPEAKER

I am honored to present an able, honest, and courageous champion of labor whose wise counsel and deep understanding of human problems have been invaluable to the labor movement through the years. In the labor movement, where the cause of freedom is treasured, his name is held in admiration and respect. We can never forget his service to our cause, nor the statesmanlike quality of his leadership. Mr. Vincent Vinston.

LABOR DAY ADDRESS

Labor Day brings back memories of the days not long ago when the rights of workingmen meant little more than the right to work long hours at brutally low pay in unsanitary and dangerous factories and plants—with illness, old age and unemployment constant threats to be dreaded. In those days the banding together of workingmen to improve their lot was looked upon as a "conspiracy" and was punished by the courts as such. In time, the courts gradually found labor organizations and their aims legal, and so free of the charge of criminal conspiracy. Yet the road was hard and stormy. There have been great strikes since then in many industries. There have been many labor martyrs.

The influence and prestige of labor has advanced considerably in the last century. Peter McGuire wrote, "There was a time and it was not too many years ago when the trade union and the labor movement of America were too insignificant for president, governors, mayors, city councilmen or public men to consider, much less honor. Trade unions were of no consequence; trade unionists were harmless fanatics." Now neither President, nor governor, nor mayor, nor city councilmen ignore the trade union movement in America. Indeed, the President of the United States helped dedicate the new headquarters of the merged AFL and CIO organizations in Washington, D. C. Governors and mayors now pay heed to the voice of a united labor movement of more than 20,000,000 members. Few pieces of legislation involving the social usefulness of the country are ever considered by Congress without an expression of organized labor's viewpoint on their value. Few candidates for public office take to the platform without considering the viewpoint of the millions of men and women who are members of great labor organizations.

Some may feel that Labor Day is not of great importance—that it is just another holiday. I think that we should be made to realize that Labor Day is our holiday—the holiday of the workers. It was created to focus attention to the fact that labor is part of the mass of American citizenry and not just another day off or to get away for a picnic. There should be a national demonstration by the members of organized labor to awaken interest in such an important day.

CLOSING

In these days of automobiles people can and do get away and there are a great many diversions. That is why Labor Day celebrations have been reduced to a minimum. I think we should do all in our power to restore this day as The Day of labor. We should try to re-establish the idea of Labor Day as the day of the worker so the community may know who the trade union members are. It should be a day set aside in honor of American workers. It should be an opportunity to tell everyone what contributions labor makes, apart from our trade union activities, to the community life. We should revive interest in the holiday as Labor Day, rather than just another holiday.

We will conclude by singing the National Anthem. Please rise. (*National Anthem is sung.*)

41. Bill of Rights Program

This is Bill of Rights Day, and it should be one of the biggest days of any year. It is the anniversary of the adoption of the first ten Amendments to the Constitution, known as the Bill of Rights. By the Bill of Rights we are guaranteed the most precious of liberties, freedom of speech, press and religion; the right to peaceably assemble and to petition the government, among its many privileges. Free and open bargaining between management and labor is guaranteed in the Constitution and in the Bill of Rights. Labor all over the country is celebrating this occasion. Labor has always fought vigorously against religious and racial bigotry in American life, recognizing that democracy can flourish only in a climate free from prejudice and discrimination. We recognize that racial bigotry is un-American and that our freedom can survive only in a country free from hate and discord.

Labor is also mindful of its community responsibilities. We are strong supporters of sound programs required for community progress in such vital areas as education, housing, economic development, recreational facilities, and health and welfare services. Any program involving advocacy of the dignity of man will receive our whole-hearted support.

Reverend Theodore Strum will deliver the invocation.

PRAYER

Almighty God, our Heavenly Father who at Sinai established the code by which all laws, moral, municipal and ecclesiastical, must be measured, who in Thyself are justice, truth and mercy, we beseech Thee to inspire all the law-makers with right and true ideals. Make them to see that in all of their efforts for the administration of the law they may set before their eyes a justice which is even and applicable to all sorts and conditions of men. Inspire them to temper justice with mercy that in the end the welfare of their fellow-citizens, rather than their own individual successes and triumphs, may be secured. We beseech Thee to direct us in all our doings with Thy most gracious favor, that we may glorify Thy holy name, and, finally, through Thy mercy, may obtain everlasting life. Amen!

INTRODUCING SPEAKER

The principal address of the day will be delivered by one who is a vigorous champion of justice and equality for all citizens and is devoted to promoting better group relations. He is a courageous and gallant fighter for a cause which is dear to the hearts of all who believe in the democratic ideal of equality among men. He is fair-minded and of unimpeachable integrity. He has devoted his life to the service of others. His deepest concern is to see the achievement of a world in which men could live together in peace and dignity.

It is an unusual honor to introduce to you Senator Seymour Smith.

ADDRESS

As trade unionists and as Americans we have a tremendous job to do in these difficult days. When the authors of the Constitution gave us this valuable charter which we call the Bill of Rights, they knew that the liberties granted us could be made good only in blood and suffering. As a people we may again be called to such trials. Certainly, we must not permit ourselves to grow soft or careless. We have a glorious inheritance in America. We have it partly because men have laid down their lives for what they believed to be true. Founders of the labor movement in America have died to preserve freedom for us.

Powerful forces are at work in the world—both to preserve and to destroy our liberties. There is need to be alert in order to preserve our heritage of liberty, and hand it down to the next generation as we have received it.

Every human being has an inherent dignity and integrity which must be respected and safeguarded. The welfare of the individual is the final goal of group life. Each of us, to be secure in the rights he wishes for himself, must be willing not only to respect but to fight for the rights of other men.

What matters most in this observance is that it is a reminder that the Bill of Rights is alive and that this historic document has so much vitality it will continue to live for generations to come. We are a young nation. The immortal dream of freedom, transmitted into our living Constitution, can survive only as generations of Americans believe in it, work for it, and dedicate themselves to it. It is that fundamental philosophy which says that the most obscure boy or girl shall not be denied the right to succeed because of religion or racial extraction. That is my definition of individual liberty and personal freedom. It is the guiding star and cornerstone of this great labor movement which serves ten million men and women working in the United States.

It must not be permitted to slip from our minds that a very few years ago one demagogue had attained such power that many people were afraid to express freely their convictions and speak their minds. We must not forget how close we ourselves have been walking on the brink of tyranny. We must not forget the horrors of Buchenwald.

May I express to your Chairman my grateful thanks for his invitation to address this distinguished body, and to each of you my gratitude for your courteous attention. Thank you very much.

CLOSING

The programs of the labor unions have the cooperation of religious leaders of all faiths, public leaders of widely assorted views, civic bodies and government authorities. Our aim is essentially educational—to solve the central problem of human rights with a mature, responsible, and patient effort to reaffirm and strengthen the religious values, ethical precepts, and respect for others which are implicit in our democracy.

Meetings such as this flourish and feed the flames of

freedom. They add substance to the hope for freedom through knowledge and free exchange of ideas.

Our labor institutions have done much to enlarge the meaning of human freedom and to enrich the meaning of true democracy. They have fought abuses in every form as they have fought every form of infringement of the basic rights of citizens guaranteed by the Constitution and by the Bill of Rights. To preserve and extend our fundamental democratic heritage, they have sought to promote the principle and practice of equal rights for all in every aspect of life in America. They have also struggled to maintain and strengthen the basic freedoms of speech, conscience, and assembly, and to give full effect to the right to petition.

42. Memorial Services

OPENING

Our Union has set aside this month to honor our departed members. In honoring them, we are carrying on a great tradition. In the inevitable course of events our membership loses each year men whom it esteems and loves. We treasure our remembrance of them and have the consolation of knowing that even after death their memories endure to stimulate the noble traditions of our Union.

On this occasion we pause to reflect on the many achievements of our departed brothers. They helped make the glorious history of this Union. Today we are reaping the rewards of their steadfast loyalty to the principles of unionism and the many sacrifices they made. It is up to us who are here today to see that this great organization for which they laid the foundation continues to be worthy of their wonderful achievements.

INTRODUCING CLERGYMAN

Our guest clergyman has given great leadership to the community not only as a churchman but also as a civic leader. He is an enemy of prejudice and a firm supporter of the practices and policies which this organization advocates. He practices what he preaches. He has the interest of the entire community and its citizens close to his heart. We will be honored by having the benediction given by Reverend Fulton Flood.

BENEDICTION

Infinite and Eternal God, Father of all men, our Guide and our Strength: we bow before Thee in this moment filled with memories that bring us to gratitude for this invested life. May this family of labor be Thy humble servant and so attain to the glory designed for them. Amen!

INTRODUCING PUBLIC OFFICIAL

I take pleasure in presenting to you one who is close to

the labor movement. He has demonstrated a profound understanding of labor problems and has always fought bigotry with zest, courage, and imagination. He has our deep respect and admiration, for he is a warm, sincere person. Mayor Samuel Smith.

EULOGY

It is the purpose of this impressive ceremony to honor the memory of those sterling members of a great Union who made the supreme sacrifice in the service of their country and their fellow-men. The men whom we honor today have gone on to walk side by side with other great men of your Union. By their devotion to the interests of their fellow-men they carried the banner of the Union through a half-century of progress to the outstanding position in trade unionism that it holds today.

By virtue of membership in your Union today you have working conditions that make it possible to enjoy a more abundant life. You have security. You have an opportunity as free union men to exert a reasonable and powerful influence in your industry. You have all these things because of the progressive and intelligent application of a principle which is the very foundation of democracy—your inalienable privilege of joining hands with your fellow-workers to guarantee a Bill of Rights for labor.

Your Union has a wonderful history. Your founders had little to start with except courage and faith in an ideal. When your Union was founded working conditions were extremely harsh. After years of sacrifice your Union finally attained the purpose of its formation.

It is up to you to see that the achievements of the past shall be the basis for further success in the future. A great opportunity lies ahead to continue your high standards. You are a part of a vast and expanding industry that has been a pillar in the American way of life—and by upholding that way of life you will have a glorious future.

ROLL CALL

The officers and members of the Union will rise and stand for a moment out of respect to the memory of our dear, departed brothers whose names will be read by the Secretary. (*Reads roll.*)

CLOSING BENEDICTION

O Lord, Almighty and Eternal God, Who has domination over all men, may He look down with favor upon the workers of our land. Grant that the decisions of their leaders may always be just because so much depends upon them for the happiness and welfare of our people. Amen!

Index